THE
COMPLETE
BOOK
OF

CURTAINS
AND
DRAPES

Lady
Caroline Wrey

THE
COMPLETE
BOOK
OF
CURTAINS
AND
DRAPES

Lady

Caroline Wrey

Century
London Sydney Auckland Johannesburg

Editor Sally Harding

Designer Polly Dawes

Copy Editor Eleanor Van Zandt

Picture Researcher Shona Wood

Artwork Vana Haggerty

First published in 1991 by Random Century Ltd,
Random Century House, 20 Vauxhall Bridge Road,
London SW1V 2SA, England

Random Century Australia (Pty) Ltd,
20 Alfred Street, Milsons Point, Sydney,
New South Wales 2061, Australia

Random Century New Zealand Ltd,
18 Poland Road, Glenfield,
Auckland 10, New Zealand

Random Century South Africa (Pty) Ltd,
PO Box 377, Bergvlei,
2012 South Africa

British Library Cataloguing
in Publication Data
Wrey, Lady Caroline
The complete book of curtains and drapes.
I. Title
746.9

ISBN 0 7126 4697 3

Set in Garamond by Rowland Phototypesetting Ltd,
Bury St Edmunds, Suffolk

Printed and bound by Tien Wah Press, Singapore

CONTENTS

Chapter One

CREATING THE
PERFECT LOOK

Curtains are one of the most crucial aspects of the interior decoration of any home.
Because a window is so often the major focal point within a room, its treatment
deserves careful thought and attention. Although you might be tempted to make
your own curtains (also sometimes called 'draperies' in the United States), you may
well feel that you lack the necessary confidence, essential skills and trade secrets. In
this book I teach you all you need to know to make your own stunning, thoroughly
professional curtains – beginning, in this chapter, with creating
your own window treatment designs.

The art of curtain making
I am passionate about curtains. To me, curtain making is a highly creative and relaxing occupation and can give great pleasure and satisfaction. Once you have set yourself up with the simple equipment required, chosen the material for a particular room and decided on the design, you can have so much *fun* making your curtains.

Never look upon a project as daunting – it is essentially easy and requires only the most basic sewing skills. Nor should you ever feel put off by the sheer volume of fabric, as the only trick to handling large amounts of material is having the right tools (see page 30).

Approaching curtain designing
To me a window is like a face and therefore needs dressing with immense care to create the perfect balance. I feel that the window belongs, primarily, to the mistress of the house; it is her prerogative to do with it, within reason, exactly what she likes. It is a great excuse to create something of beauty – something extremely pleasing to the eye in every respect.

When walking into a house, with a view to creating perfect window treatments throughout, you will find that there are many existing limitations, within which you must work. Each room has a different function; therefore it demands and deserves an individual treatment, specifically designed for that room alone.

Your first creative choice is to decide what visual impact or atmosphere you are trying to achieve in a particular room:

– Peaceful simplicity
– Comfortable abundance and relaxation
– Discreet subtlety
– Immense luxury
– Bold drama

Keep in mind which of the above qualities, or a combination of which of the above qualities, you are aiming for while you are designing your curtains and pelmets.

Whatever you are trying to achieve in your window treatment always consider using a pelmet (called a 'valance' or 'cornice' in the United States depending on the style). I like to use a pelmet whenever possible because it finishes off the window with such style, however simple or elaborate the pelmet may be.

THE 7-PRONG DESIGN PLAN

As a guide to designing window treatments, I have developed what I call the '7-Prong Plan'. It covers the seven aspects of your window treatment that you must consider *simultaneously* when composing your design:

1. **Curtain material**
2. **Direction of window**
3. **Light obstruction and view**
4. **Period of house**
5. **Function of room**
6. **Trimmings**
7. **Overall style of room**

By ignoring any one of the seven parts of the plan you will risk creating an unsettling effect.

1. Curtain material
Your choice of curtain material is largely a question of your own taste, but keep in mind that you are choosing something that you will have to live with for a long time. When choosing material, unroll a long length, step back from it and look at it from a distance. This is how you will be seeing it in a room – not up close the way you would a dress fabric.

In fact, colours you like for clothing may not be the same ones you like for soft furnishings. For instance, I find primary colours very harsh to look at in window treatments, but lovely to wear. Primary colours have no scope in interior design and appear soulless.

Softer colours, colours more 'toned down' than primary colours, will be the ones that will be a joy to live with for a long time. Other colours to avoid, aside from primary colours, are what I call the 'sludge' colours, such as camel and brown. They will bring no life at all into your room.

But choosing colour, texture and print design are dependent not only on your own taste. They must be considered in relation to all of the other aspects of the 7-Prong Plan.

2. Direction of window
One of these factors is the direction that the window faces: north, south, east or west. The 'cold' colours – blues, pale greens, and whites, for example – will be suitable for windows facing in certain directions: and the 'warm' colours – pinks, reds, golds, yellows, for example – for windows facing in other directions.

Depending on where you are in the world, there will be 'light' directions and 'dark' directions. In the Northern Hemisphere, south and west are the two 'light' and 'warm' directions. This is because a window facing south or west receives far stronger and more golden sunlight than it would if it were facing north or east. Also a room facing south or west in Great Britain is bound to be warmer than one facing north or east, because of the temperature of the wind. In light rooms virtually both 'warm' and 'cold' colours will be possible.

If, however, your window is facing a direction that will make a room cold, you should avoid fabrics in cold colours and go for the warmer colours. Equally, if it is not a particularly light room, be cautious about using too many dark colours. This may also influence your choice of fabric texture (chintz reflects light better than linen, for example) and window treatment (a heavy, deep pelmet will have a darkening effect).

3. Light obstruction and view
When you look at a window treatment in the room, you can never divorce it from the view filling the whole window space. Therefore you must always think of the curtains and pelmets in permanent conjunction with what is outside. For example, if a huge cedar tree or a tall yew hedge is dominating the view, you will have a predominance of deep, blackish green. This should influence your material choice, in terms of its colours. You will need a strong contrast.

Both floral and striped chintzes will provide a good frame for a rural

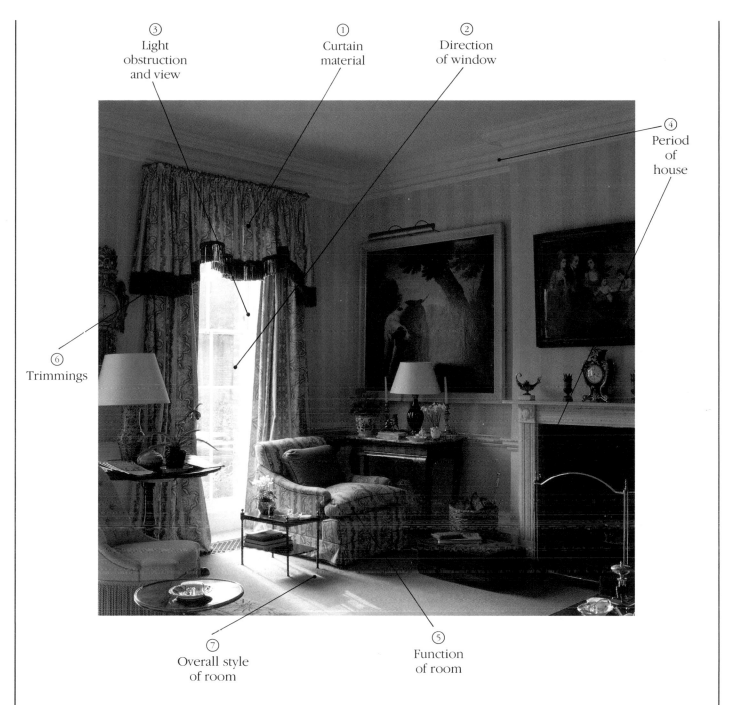

③ Light obstruction and view

① Curtain material

② Direction of window

④ Period of house

⑥ Trimmings

⑦ Overall style of room

⑤ Function of room

This window treatment (above) is successful because all of the aspects of the 7-Prong Plan have been carefully considered.

1. **Curtain material:** *The deep dusky rose pink is a marvellous colour for old-master type paintings and for antique furniture. The warmth of the colour and the timeless, classical quality of the material make this window treatment very easy to live with.*
2. **Direction of window:** *Because the window is east-facing, the choice of a warm colour is appropriate. Also the*
bullion fringe allows extra light to filter through.*
3. **Light obstruction and view:** *There are no obstructions here to reduce the light; and the view of pink brickwork blends perfectly with the choice of material.*
4. **Period of house:** *The classical shape and details of the pelmet fit in well with the classical period of the room. The proportions of the pelmet also suit the proportions of the room.*
5. **Function of room:** *The treatment exudes qualities that are essential for*
a drawing room – elegance, comfort and luxury. It also helps make the room cosy and inviting.*
6. **Trimmings:** *The bullion fringe gives the final impact to the overall design by accentuating the serpent shape of the pelmet. The contrast binding at the top lends perfect balance.*
7. **Overall style of room:** *All of the contributing factors of the window treatment tie in beautifully with the whole room. The window is just as it should be – a wonderful focal point but it does not 'jump out' at you.*

fashioned flower prints made up into swags and tails would look very out of place.

Basically, you should try to complement the architectural style with the window treatment. For a beautiful gothic line, for example, your treatment should either follow the gothic curves or else hang completely clear of the window so that none of its elegant lines are obscured. In a modern house stick with the more modern-style chintzes that are available.

5. Function of room

Before you start designing, have absolutely clear in your mind what the room is to be used for. To illustrate this point, let us now mentally take a walk through a house:

Entrance hall or landing

The hall is a reception area in which, on the whole, you spend very little time. But it is the first 'room' you walk into; therefore it can be fairly influential in setting the mood and pace, in terms of window treatments, for the rest of the house.

I feel that this is a place where you can easily afford to be bold and dramatic in your treatment. The point is that a hall is unlikely to contain a huge amount of furniture or ornaments with which you have to harmonize your treatment. Because the window treatment in an entrance hall is a fairly isolated affair, and one that you tend to pass by rather than sit with, you should try to create here something with quite an impact.

What is true for an entrance hall is equally true for a landing. If the windows in your hall or landing are small, you may even want to make them look bigger by giving them an emphatic treatment, such as floor-length curtains.

The perfect green facing in this elegant swags and tails window treatment (above) shows the importance of choosing just the right contrasting colours for the overall design.

The lavish effect of these stunning smocked-headed silk curtains (right) is achieved by lining them in heavy interlining.

scene. I find, however, that something to avoid in the country is a print produced in colours that deviate strongly from nature – like blue leaves, for example.

I think that in town houses it is lovely to be reminded of the country as often as possible, and this can be achieved very successfully by making use of those heavenly, old-fashioned flower/leaf prints. Chintzes in spring colours will evoke country living.

If your city dwelling is high up and you have a long view which is mostly a skyscape – a neutral backdrop to your window – any number of colours and prints could be used. If, on the other hand, the view is terribly unappealing, you may want to use net curtains, called 'sheers', to cover the view but let in the lovely light.

4. Period of house

It is worth taking into consideration the date of the house you are working with before you set your heart on certain designs for a window treatment. For example, let's say you adore serpent-tail pelmets (see page 90), but live in a seventeenth-century farmhouse with 2.20m (6ft 10in) ceilings. The two simply do not go together. Fortunately, however, there are so many different and attractive pelmet and trimming designs that there is absolutely no need to fall hopelessly in love with designs with big drops and curves.

Swags and tails (see page 91), and serpent-tail pelmets, are wonderfully suited to the larger proportions of Georgian, Regency and Victorian architecture. Equally, in a house of a very modern design, both inside and out, those beautiful old-

Drawing room/sitting room

The drawing room, or – in a less imposing house – the sitting or living room, for me conjures up glamour, luxury, elegance and extreme comfort; and you should design your window treatments accordingly. In this respect an important rule to remember is: LENGTH IS ELEGANCE. So aim for floor-length curtains and the most lavish pelmet you can successfully carry off in a particular room.

However, I am all for keeping bows out of the drawing room, and if you are using frills as a trimming, why not pleat them rather than gather them? Pleated frills (see page 21) are elegant and therefore more suitable for a drawing room than gathered frills, which are 'pretty' and better suited to a bedroom.

In terms of materials, very beautiful chintzes or silks (wild [U.S. 'raw'] or corded) are both excellent choices for drawing rooms. Even if you choose a very inexpensive silk, by the time you have interlined it with medium- or heavyweight interlining, trimmed it beautifully and given it a superb pelmet, it will look the most lavish thing ever. (See *Curtain materials* page 18.)

Study or office

The window treatment for a man's study or office should preserve the room's essentially masculine character. It is therefore advisable to avoid too many curves and frills and, instead, go for very organized, tailored pleats, whether they are French, goblet or box pleats. A chintz or a linen in a lovely rich, bold colour – such as tomato red – would add the finishing touch.

Whether it is a man's or a woman's study, the room must be one that is easy to work in. You will need to let in plenty of light, so if it is a north- or east-facing room, go easy on the depth of the pelmet.

Dining room

The dining room is a room that you will entertain guests in for hours on end, so it is fun, yet again, to create quite an impact. I feel that in the dining room you should perhaps have something other than chintz. The logic behind this is that you are

bound to be using chintz in many other areas of the house, so why not do something rather different here?

Think beyond chintzes to linens and silks, and, because the room will usually be occupied after dark, use warm colours. To enhance both the curtains and the pelmet, light them unobtrusively with uplighters placed on the floor. If you do this, the whole window treatment will come alive, especially if the only other sources of light in your dining

room are candles, picture lights or wall sconces.

Kitchen

If you do not have a 'farmhouse' type kitchen – the type with exposed brickwork, pine dressers and hanging baskets – then you may have a very smart fitted kitchen which is all fairly high-tech. Curtains for these modern kitchens should, I feel, 'dissolve' a little of the endless 'high-tech' atmosphere, with all its

right angles unavoidably created by the countless units, tiles and work surfaces. For this purpose I love to design Austrian blinds (see page 102) for kitchens. They have such bounce and depth and can introduce curves into a room basically devoid of them.

Bedroom
A more reticent mood of peace and tranquillity should prevail in the bedroom. But the bedroom is the

place where you have the excuse to execute very 'pretty' design treatments – bows and gathered frills being the details that I have in mind.

In children's bedrooms, Austrian blinds for girls and Roman blinds for boys are extremely suitable, since they take up very little space. The wall space under the window is then free for bookshelves, toy boxes or other pieces of furniture. I also think it is a mistake to make any

These dining room curtains (above) have a fixed, or static, heading of elegant mini-goblet pleats. (See page 60 for full instructions on how to make goblet-pleated headings on your curtains.)

The striped material of the curtains ties in well with the style of this dining room (facing page). The knotted rope detail along the top of the box-pleated pelmet adds presence and a touch of elegance.

child's room too babyish. They grow up into huge six-year-olds incredibly fast, and whereas babies don't care at all what curtains they have, six-year-olds certainly do. It is an awful waste of time, money and effort to have to replace the dear little hopping bunnies.

Tartans are good for boys' rooms and soft pretty colours for girls' rooms. I have wonderful memories of the chintz curtains in my room as a child, which had lovely yellow hammers flying through apple blossom.

Bathroom

As with kitchens, I have a great desire to 'dissolve' the clinical atmosphere of a bathroom. If you have the type of window that can 'take' a floor-length curtain, then seize the opportunity. I think it is delightful to make a bathroom as pretty and as glamorous as possible, so that it is a real pleasure to be in.

Thick floor-length curtains will naturally exclude all draughts. The architect is bound to have position-ed a radiator under the window (they always do) but this must be ignored! You must avoid short curtains whenever possible.

If a short curtain is absolutely necessary – because there is a basin under the window, for example – then use an Austrian blind (see page 102), which looks extremely pretty in a bathroom. Remember that it is terribly nice to dress and bath in a room that both looks and feels warm and cosy.

6. Trimmings

To me trimmings on your pelmets are the final icing on the cake. They are the detail on your window treatment that will cause the greatest impact and convey the message of the particular shape and rhythm of the pelmet. Without trimmings your window treatment will lose half of its effect.

The sky is the limit where trim-mings are concerned. Those you

The gentle serpent shape of this pelmet (right) is so suitable for a bedroom and for fairly wide windows. The stand-up at the top of the pelmet effec-tively balances the serpent.

choose depend entirely on personal taste and budget (see page 20 for how to make various handmade trimmings).

7. Overall style of the room
However simple or elaborate it is, the window treatment you have created must be in harmony with the rest of the room. Although the window is arguably the focal point of the room, its style should echo the overall style of the rest of the room and not dominate it. What you should aim for is an equilibrium between the style of the room and the style of the window treatment.

Although I am all for their making a certain impact on the viewer, your curtains and pelmets must not stand out as a foreign body or misfit. For example, if the general decoration of your room – pictures, furniture, carpets, lamps and so on – is predominantly modern, then a very old-fashioned print in swags and tails would probably look somewhat out of place.

Your final design
If you have taken into account all of the elements in the 7-Prong Design Plan, your window-treatment design is bound to be successful. You can

Without trimmings – ready-made (above) or handmade – your window treatment will lose half its effect. The sky is the limit for trimmings and those you choose depend entirely on personal taste and budget.

now approach the task of making curtains and pelmets with enough confidence to make it a very enjoyable experience.

Chapter Two

MATERIALS AND TRIMMINGS

Once you have followed the 7-Prong Design Plan in Chapter 1 you will have decided
on your window treatment. You should also have a good idea of the colour of the
material you are looking for. In this chapter I guide you through your search for
the perfect curtain material and instruct you on the types of lining and interlining
to choose. I also give you step-by-step instructions on how to make handmade
trimmings which will put the icing on the cake and give your pelmet
design the impact it deserves.

CURTAIN MATERIALS

Your ultimate choice of material is obviously crucial to the overall success of the finished window treatment. First, however, you must decide what sort of look you are trying to create – whether it be something classical in spirit or perhaps something more contemporary. This decision has a bearing on the choice of fibre as well as the choice of colour and print (see page 8).

The range of furnishing fabric available for curtains is enormous. To my mind, however, if you are trying to achieve a window treatment that will be truly successful, stick to natural fibres. Synthetic materials may in some cases be cheaper, but this in the long run may be a false economy. Nothing can compare to natural fibres for hanging, feel, durability and beauty. And it is certainly good to keep in mind, when using the large quantities of fabric that curtains require, that natural fibres are environmentally friendly.

When I choose curtain fabrics, I make my choice from one of the following categories – chintz, linen, damask and silk. This may seem to narrow the field unduly, but you will never regret having made curtains in one of these lovely natural fibres. They will be a joy to live with for many years. I often think of my grandmother's damask curtains, which still look wonderful after fifty years.

Chintz

Chintz is an extremely popular material to use for curtaining. Originally 'chintz' referred to the painted or stained calico made in India. Today, it is the name given to glazed cotton cloth, usually printed with coloured designs.

There are many modern and old chintz prints on the market – all with their own individual beauty. Chintz has the most fantastic quality of having amazing body, given to it by its glaze. It is a joy to work with, since it is so pliable and manageable in situations where you want details on window treatments to have bounce and life (for example, gathered pelmets of any kind, choux rosettes and Austrian blinds). Chintz also has the lovely characteristic of reflecting the light.

Linen

Because it is not glazed, linen has a limited ability to reflect light compared to chintz. This is a point worth remembering if you are considering using a dark-coloured linen in a north-facing or an east-facing room.

There are some very beautiful linens to be found. They look superb in window treatments and appear so original, compared to chintz, which is used far more frequently.

Damask

Damask is a marvellous, timeless material which has been used very successfully for centuries. It is a 'reversible' figured material in which a matt design is executed in the 'wrong' side of a satin weave, the right side of which forms the background. The two weaves are reversed on the wrong side of the material.

Damask was originally woven in silk, but later in linen and cotton. Its name comes from the fact that early damask came from Damascus. Still extremely easy to obtain, damask looks superb on windows – especially when the pelmet is a shaped, stiffened one. A shaped, stiff pelmet shows off beautifully the intricate designs woven into the solid-colour damask.

Silk

Silks come in many forms – from fairly lightweight wild silks to fairly heavyweight corded silks. Since it is easy to find many silks that are either less expensive than many chintzes or no more so, silk should be used more often in curtaining.

Silk curtains and pelmets have a great impact, especially when lit from the floor, even in the most basic fashion (see page 12). When lit like this at night, the whole window treatment comes alive in the most gorgeous way.

LININGS AND INTERLININGS

Most curtain materials will need to be lined and interlined for the best effect to be achieved. The old-fashioned method of lining and interlining curtains has never been surpassed for creating perfect curtains. Using the best lining and interlining material will give your curtains a rich depth, producing lovely folds which hang beautifully. Remember that thick curtains will look sumptuous and, when drawn, will flow with a fluid movement.

Plain linings

For lining material, a pure cotton sateen is preferred and is the most widely available curtain lining on the market. It usually comes either 120cm (48in) or 137cm (54in) wide, and it is worth buying the wider lining. Although it is slightly more expensive per metre (yard) than the narrower lining, you will probably find that your chosen curtain material is nearer to 137cm (54in) wide than 120cm (48in). It will therefore save you the effort of joining all those panels in the narrower width in order to make it up to the correct finished width for the curtains.

Bear in mind, when working with cotton sateen lining, that it is not a strong quality fibre, so it should be used only as a lining.

Sateen lining comes in a wide range of colours; however, neutral colours – white, ivory, ecru and beige – are the ones most commonly used.

My clients sometimes request a white lining for their curtains, but if the choice is left to me I advise that ivory is the best colour to use for most curtains and pelmets. It is much more pleasing to the eye than a stark, cold white; it does not look as dirty as white will after a few years of hanging, and it will also not show discolouration from exposure to light in the way white does.

If for some reason ivory is not available, then ecru should be your second choice. Like ivory it is more gentle on the eye than white and doesn't have its disadvantages.

Beige lining is rarely recommended. It is very dark and therefore discolours easily from the light. It would also show through any of the white-background chintzes and spoil their appearance.

*The look you are trying to achieve –
whether classical in spirit or more
contemporary – has a bearing on the
ultimate choice of material and trimmings (above).*

Coloured linings

Although coloured linings look very
pretty when you see them on the
bolts, they are not such a good idea
because their dyes are not strong.
The sun is capable of draining the
colour out of a curtain lining in a
few years, especially if it is facing the
south or west. This is terribly
disappointing after going to all the
effort and expense involved in
curtain making. If you are
determined to have a coloured
lining, you would do better to
choose a very cheap, thin, plain
chintz (see page 128 for list of
suppliers). The dyes in these
chintzes are relatively colourfast.

If you are thinking of using a
coloured lining for a bedroom
curtain in order to keep the
morning sun out, why not order a
coloured roller blind instead?

Synthetic linings

It is best to avoid using synthetic
linings, as they have no redeeming
features. There are certain synthetic
linings that are sold as a single
alternative to the double combination of both lining and interlining.
But these fabrics are solid and
graceless. I would strongly advise
you not to use them.

Another synthetic lining which
you may be tempted to use is
blackout lining. It is very expensive,
but it does have the ability to black
out the room totally at any hour of
the day. It is a very strange fabric
which is plastic on the back and a
woven textile on the front. If you
use it as a lining on its own, without
interlining, it gives the curtains a
thin, hard, stiff quality and a papery
look. Using it with an interlining is a
better alternative, but this then
makes the whole window treatment
very heavy in both appearance and
weight. Again, I advise against it. If
you want to cut out light totally, use
a roller blind specially designed for
that purpose.

Medium-weight interlining

Interlining comes in various
thicknesses, but the medium weight
is the best for almost all curtain
materials, including all chintzes,
linens, damasks and heavy silks.

Medium-weight interlining, also
called 'bump' (see *Glossary* on page
130 for American equivalent), , is a
multi-purpose thick, furry cotton
fabric. It is used for curtains and
pelmets, as well as for stuffing such
things as plaited or ruched tie-backs
or goblet pleats.

Bump has wonderful qualities that
I never tire of praising. It has a soft
yet firm body that makes your
curtains and pelmets look heavy,

thick and lavish. It also protects the print of the material from the sun, insulates the room beautifully, and helps the fluid movement of the curtains as they are drawn backwards and forwards across the window.

In addition, medium-weight interlining is incredibly easy to work with. It frays very little and is very manageable when being moved, reacting much like a soft, light, firm woolly blanket. But *beware of your clothes* – bump will leave a dreadful white fluff on everything, which is a special disaster on navy blue and on black!

Heavy interlining
I rarely use heavy interlining, except in three specific situations. Firstly when designing curtains that need to look very, very thick and lavish, I will use heavy interlining as a special luxury. Secondly, most silks are fairly thin and will need that extra body that a heavy bump will give. And thirdly, certain unglazed cottons will require a heavier interlining because they tend to crease more easily than chintz.

Of course, in kitchens a heavy interlining should not be used even for the fabrics mentioned above, because it would give a much too weighty effect.

Lightweight interlining
Lightweight interlining, or 'domette' (see *Glossary* on page 130 for a suggested American equivalent), is essential in caught-up pelmets (see page 82), since they must retain a 'light' look. Domette is also used for ruched swags and tails (see page 92) which would not hang as well if they were interlined with medium-weight interlining.

I have only ever used lightweight interlining in curtains when I have wanted them to look very light and airy. This is usually when designing curtains to be used in a country with a hot climate.

Despite the fact that you may want the light to come through the curtain material, it is imperative to interline most curtains in some way or other, even if only with a lightweight interlining, or the sun will rot them all too quickly.

HANDMADE TRIMMINGS
As I mentioned in Chapter 1, trimmings are the component in curtain designing whose impact should never be underestimated. The joy of making trimmings yourself is that not only is it a hugely creative pastime, but it will also use up those fabric remnants cut off when matching the pattern repeat and save you the expense of ready-made trimmings.

Instructions are given here for the frills that I find the most versatile and effective. Commercially made fan-edges, fringes, bullions (see *Glossary* on page 130) and the like, are elegant but not cheap, and can be hard to find.

Making trimmings is incredibly popular in the curtain classes I give. The process seems to give enjoyment because it is so quickly learned and because the resulting frills are so professional-looking and effective.

Frills and the pelmet drop
I always include handmade frills in the total finished drop of a pelmet, as they are a solid edge. Bullions, however, I tend to add on as an extra to the finished length of the drop, because a lot of light comes through them.

Choosing materials for frills
The easiest material to use for frills is chintz, because it is so easy to fold and gather. But you should always match your frill fabric to your main curtain fabric, using chintz to edge chintz, silk to edge silk and so on. If your main fabric is a print, use either the same print or a rich solid colour for the frill. For solid-coloured curtains you can, again, either match the frill to the curtain colour or use a contrast.

Always use matching thread when machine stitching your frills.

Set-on or inset frills
The handmade frills that follow are predominantly used for pelmets (see page 71), but can also be used on the *leading edges* (the centre vertical edges of a pair of curtains) which may have a fixed head and no pelmet. This type of curtain is not drawn but remains in a fixed, tied-back position, so the leading edge can become a very prominent feature if adorned with a frill.

Any of the frills that follow can be made so that they can be inset between the lining and the pelmet material, or so that they can be 'set-on' the edge of an already-hemmed pelmet. Frills to be inset will have a raw edge at the top, whereas frills to be 'set-on' the edge will have top and bottom edges which are both turned back.

One advantage of a set-on frill is that you can create, along the top of the edging, a narrow little frill called a 'stand-up'.

Cutting and joining frill pieces
Frill pieces should always be cut on the straight grain of the material. This may be the crosswise grain (selvedge to selvedge) or the lengthwise grain (parallel to the selvedge). Straight-bladed cutting-out shears are used except where a raw edge is not to be turned under; in such cases pinking shears are indicated in the instructions.

If the frill material is a print, do not attempt to match the pattern when joining seams. It is totally unnecessary. Over such a short distance a mismatch will never be noticed – especially once the strip is gathered or pleated.

Machine-gathered inset frill
As a trimming, the handmade machine-gathered frill has a soft and subtle character.

You will see that the gathering is done by hand as the strip of material is fed through the machine. The technique used in dressmaking of pulling long, loose machine stitches is not possible when making metres (yards) of trimming. Evening up the gathers would be very time-consuming and the threads would inevitably break at some point while being pulled over the long lengths needed for the frills.

Gathering while machine stitching is an easy technique to pick up and needs only a little practice on scraps of material.

I recommend a 6cm (2¼in)-deep finished gathered frill for pelmets with a drop ranging from 30cm to 45cm (12in to 18in).

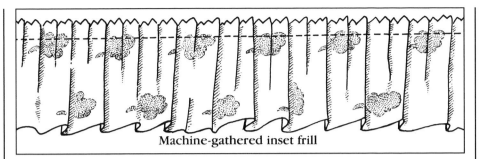

Machine-gathered inset frill

Making the frill

1 For a finished frill 6cm (2¼in) deep, cut strips of material 15cm (5½in) wide. This will allow for a 1.5cm (½in) final seam allowance along the top of the doubled-over material. Cut enough strips for the entire frill, allowing 2½ times the finished edge of the pelmet to be frilled. For example, if the lower edge of your finished pelmet is 4.8m (15ft 7½in), allow approximately 12m (13yd) of strips.

2 Join all the strips together end to end with 1.5cm (½in) seams, and press the seams open. Remember that it is totally unnecessary to pattern match.

3 Fold the joined strip in half lengthwise with wrong sides and raw edges together. Do not press the fold yet, and do not pin. Turn back 1cm (⅜in) into the folded strip at the end you are starting from. Then machine stitch along the length of the strip 1cm (⅜in) from the raw edge. Do not turn back the raw edge at the other end of the strip. This will be finished off when the frill is stitched to the pelmet. Now press.

4 Machine gather along the strip by making little tucks in the material continuously, one after another, as the material is fed through the machine. The stitches should run alongside (and just below) the stitches along the top of the frill. The trick in gathering is to use your two middle fingers to feed the material, using more pressure on the right hand, which is on the seam allowance. It is essential, especially with chintz, to lick your two fingers occasionally so that they grip. Stop and start the machine continually, as you make the little tucks (see

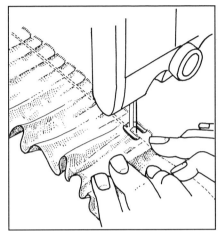

above). *Do not press a machine-gathered frill after gathering.*

5 Measure the finished frill to ensure that the frill is long enough for the pelmet (it will be trimmed to fit). Place the frill on the lower edge of the pelmet fabric, with raw edges and right sides together and with the finished end of the frill 4cm (1½in) from the end of the pelmet material. Pin only the first few centimetres (inches) to get the work started. (Pinning the entire frill to the pelmet is unnecessary.) With the frill on top, machine stitch it to the pelmet along the previously worked stitching on the frill, ending 4cm (1½in) from the end of the pelmet. A short distance before this point, cut the frill to the correct length plus 1cm (⅜in) and finish the end as for the beginning.

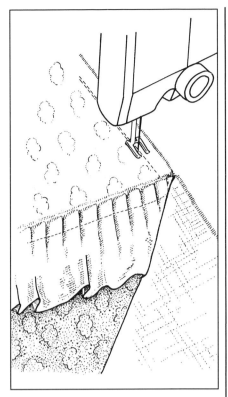

6 Now machine stitch the pelmet lining to the pelmet material, right sides together, so that the frill is sandwiched between the two fabrics. With the pelmet material facing, stitch along the previous stitches but 1.5cm (½in) from the edge (see diagram above). Open and press.

Machine-pleated inset frill
Machine pleating, as a trimming, has a far stronger, heavier and more tailored character than machine gathering. Like machine gathering, however, this frill is quick and easy to make after a little practice on scraps of fabric.

As for machine-gathered frills, I recommend a 6cm (2¼in)-deep finished pleated frill for pelmets with a drop ranging from 30cm to 45cm (12in to 18in).

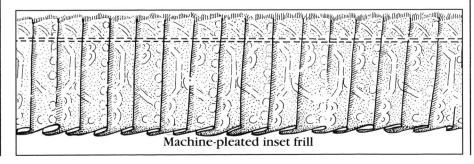

Machine-pleated inset frill

Making the frill

1 Cut and prepare the strips as for a machine-gathered frill, steps 1–3, but when cutting the strips, allow 3 times the finished pelmet width as opposed to 2½.

2 Follow step 4 of the machine-gathered frill, but instead of making little tucks, make pleats about 1cm (½in) deep continuously, one after another, along the folded strip. There is no need to measure each pleat; just fold them under each time, using your eye as the guide to width (see below).

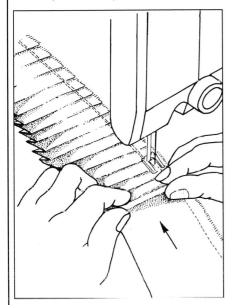

3 Having machine-pleated the frill, you must now *iron the pleats in* to make them look sharp and organized.

4 Follow steps 5 and 6 of the machine-gathered frill to sew the frill to the lower edge of the pelmet.

Double inset frill

By combining two frills of different depth, one in a solid colour and one in a print, you can create a very effective trimming. The printed frill is placed on top of the solid-coloured frill, so that the solid colour shows below the print. The solid colour should be a strong

The contrast edge on this machine-gathered inset frill (left) has been achieved by sewing on a narrow ready-made trimming, instead of by binding, although the effect is similar.

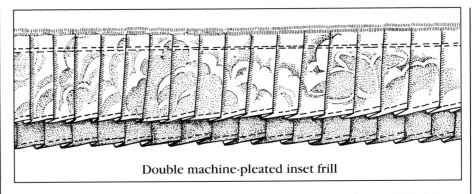

Double machine-pleated inset frill

enough contrast to show up boldly at a distance.

I recommend a 7cm (2¾in)-deep finished double gathered or pleated frill for most pelmets. The front (or narrower frill) is 1cm (⅜in) shorter than the deeper frill at the back. Because this trimming has two frills, only a single layer of fabric is used for each frill, and the lower edges are hemmed by machine.

Making the frill

1 For a finished double frill 7cm (2¾in) deep, cut strips of the *main material* 9cm (3⅜in) wide for the narrower frill which will measure 6cm (2⅜in) when finished. *Use pinking shears.* This width will allow for a 1.5cm (½in) final seam allowance along the top and 1.5cm (½in) along the bottom for turning up. Cut enough of these strips for the entire frill, allowing 2½ times the finished width of the pelmet for a gathered frill or 3 times for a pleated frill. Then join the strips end to end with 1.5cm (½in) seams, and press the seams open.

2 Cut strips of *contrasting material* for the deeper frill, and join them as for the narrower frill in step 1, but cut the strips 10cm (3¾in) wide.

3 Fold back 1.5cm (½in) at one short end of one of the two strips

and machine stitch 8mm (¼in) from the folded edge. Then turn under 1.5cm (½in) all along the lower edge of the strip and press. Machine stitch along the lower edge 8mm (¼in) from the folded edge. Press to embed the stitches.

4 Hem the second strip in the same way as the first, as in step 3. For a gathered frill, proceed to step 6.

5 For a pleated frill, pleat each of the strips separately as for the single machine-pleated frill, steps 2 and 3.

6 Place the narrower frill on top of the deeper frill, with both right sides facing upwards and raw edges together. Machine stitch the strips together 1cm (⅜in) from raw edges.

7 For a gathered frill, machine gather the doubled frill as for a single machine-gathered frill, step 4.

8 Inset the double frill into the lower edge of the pelmet as for the machine-gathered frill steps 5 and 6.

Contrast-bound set-on frill

A machine-gathered or pleated frill can be bound on the top and bottom with a contrasting colour to create two parallel lines along your pelmet. It is possible to create a similar effect by binding only the

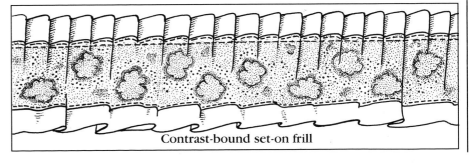

Contrast-bound set-on frill

lower edge of an inset frill and piping (U.S., 'cording') the lower edge of the pelmet, but this is a longer process.

Also, piping has the disadvantage of giving the lower edge of the pelmet a certain rigid quality. If you are using any type of softly gathered pelmet it may then not hang as gracefully as you want it to. The double bound set-on frill, on the other hand, is quicker to make and has a lovely soft, pliable quality, giving the pelmet an added dimension of delicacy.

The instructions that follow are for a 7cm (2¾in)-deep frill, which is suitable for most pelmets.

Making the frill

1 For a finished frill 7cm (2¾in) deep, cut strips of the main material 7cm (2¾in) wide. Cut enough strips for the entire frill, allowing 2½ times the finished pelmet width for a gathered frill and 3 times for a pleated frill. Then join the strips as in step 2 of a machine-gathered frill.

2 For the contrasting binding, cut strips of contrasting material 4cm (1½in) wide, *using pinking shears*. Cut and then join enough strips to make two lengths of binding: one to bind the top edge of the frill and one to bind the bottom edge.

3 Place one binding strip along one edge of the main strip with right sides and two raw edges together. Machine stitch along the length of the strips 1cm (⅜in) from the raw edges. Then sew the second contrasting strip to the other edge of the main strip in the same way. Before turning back the bindings, press the machine stitching to embed the stitches.

4 Lay the strip on the ironing board face up, and keeping the main strip flat, press back the bindings, pressing from the centre of the frill outwards. Then, using a clear plastic ruler to check width as you press, fold under the excess binding fabric to create a 1cm (⅜in) binding on the right side. Do this at both the top and bottom of the frill (see diagram above right). Do not turn under the raw edge, as the pinked

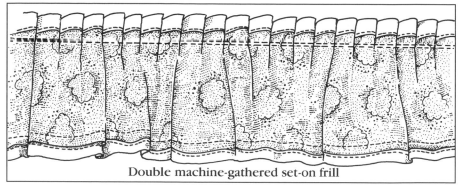

Double machine-gathered set-on frill

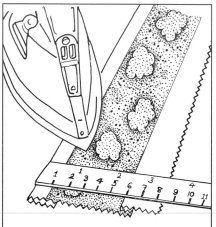

edge will be neat enough for the wrong side of the frill.

5 With the right side of the frill facing upwards, topstitch along the binding, just to one side of it, on the main fabric (see below). To ensure that the stitching is hardly visible, use thread matching the main material, and stitch as close as possible to the binding. Do this on both top and bottom of frill. Press.

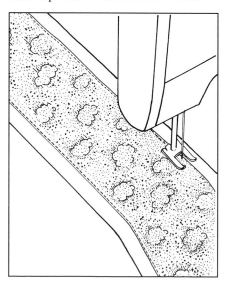

6 Folding under 1.5cm (½in) at the beginning, gather or pleat the bound frill as in step 4 of the machine-gathered frill, or pleat as in steps 2 and 3 of the machine-pleated frill, stitching 1.5cm (½in) from the top of the frill. There is now a little 'stand-up' along the top of the frill.

7 To attach the frill to the pelmet, place it along the lower edge of the finished pelmet and machine stitch, working over the gathering or pleating stitches, and cutting the frill to the correct length, and finish the end like the beginning. The set-on frill can be positioned on the edge of the finished pelmet so that most of it hangs below the edge (which will add to the overall drop of the pelmet) or so that it ends level with the pelmet's lower edge.

Double set-on frill

The double gathered or pleated set-on frill is made in much the same way as the double inset version (see page 23), but both the top and bottom edges are hemmed and the top has a little stand-up frill.

The effect of a contrast along the top and bottom of the frill, which creates a double parallel line, is similar to that of the contrast-bound set-on frill.

The instructions are for an 8cm (3⅛in)-deep frill which is suitable for many soft-gathered pelmets. The top (or narrower) frill is 1cm (⅜in) shorter than the deeper strip at both top and bottom.

This hard buckram-interfaced pelmet (right) is edged with a double machine-pleated inset frill. The shape of the pelmet was determined by the stunning trompe l'oeil print.

Making the frill

1 For a finished frill 8cm (3⅛in) deep, cut strips of *main material* 9cm (3⅜in) wide for the narrower frill, *using pinking shears*. This will allow for a 1.5cm (½in) turn-back along the top and bottom of the frill. Cut enough of these strips for the entire frill, allowing 2½ times the finished pelmet length for a gathered frill and 3 times for a pleated frill. Then join the strips end to end with 1.5cm (½in) seams, and press the seams open.

2 Cut strips of *contrasting material* for the deeper frill, and join them as for the narrower frill in step 1, but cut the strips 11cm (4⅛in) wide.

3 Fold back 1.5cm (½in) at one short end of one strip, and machine stitch 8mm (¼in) from the folded edge. Then turn under 1.5cm (½in)

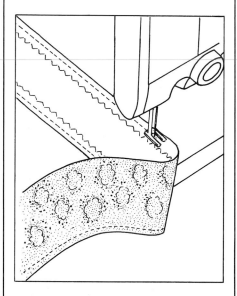

all along both the top and bottom of the strip and press. Machine stitch along both edges 8mm (¼in) from the folded edge (see above). Press to embed the stitches.

4 Hem the second strip in the same way as the first, as in step 3. For a gathered frill, proceed to step 6.

5 For a pleated frill, pleat each of the strips separately as for the single machine-pleated frill steps 2 and 3. The machine stitches should be 8mm (¼in) from the top edge of the narrower strip and 1.8cm (⅝in) from the top of the deeper strip.

6 Place the narrower frill on top of the deeper frill, with both right sides facing upwards and with the top of the narrower frill 1cm (⅜in) from the top of the deeper one. Machine stitch the strips together

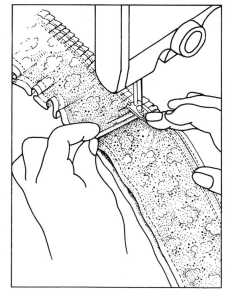

Pleated set-on frills can produce a nice tailored effect as in this Austrian blind (above). The additional detail of a knotted rope gives great presence to the design.

This is an excellent example of a contrast-bound set-on frill (right). The parallel lines of contrasting colour create a very pretty look, illustrating the impact of frills.

8mm (¼in) from the top of the narrower frill. Press to embed this last line of machine stitches.

7 For a gathered frill, machine gather the doubled frill as for a single machine-gathered frill step 4, but working over the stitches that joined the two frills (see the diagram on the left).

8 Join the finished frill to the finished pelmet as for the contrast-bound set-on frill step 8.

Permanently-pleated inset frill

The permanently-pleated frill is one of my favourite methods of trimming pelmets. To me, it is the ultimate in elegance.

To make this frill you must hem long strips of fabric and send them off to a commercial pleater (see list of suppliers on page 128) for permanent pleating. I would recommend that you ask for a 4mm (⅛in) pleating, which is usually the narrowest available and the most elegant. This narrow pleating is highly suitable for both drawing rooms and bedrooms. If you want a frill with a stronger and bolder presence, ask for 8mm (¼in) pleating.

First find out from the pleating company how long the flat frill strips should be. They will generally work with strips no longer than 10m (11yd). So if your finished pelmet will be longer than about 3m (3½yd) you may need to prepare more than one strip and sew them together after pleating.

The instructions given are for a finished inset frill of 6cm (2¼in), but of course you can create deeper frills, if necessary, or frills with a 'stand-up' at the top (see *Double gathered or pleated set-on frill* on page 24).

Making the frill

1 For a finished frill 6cm (2¼in) deep, cut strips of material 9cm (3¼in) wide, *using pinking shears*. This will allow for a 1.5cm (½in) final seam allowance along the top for setting in and 1.5cm (½in) along the bottom for turning up. Cut enough of these strips for the entire frill, allowing 3 times the finished pelmet length. Then join the strips end to end with 1.5cm (½in) seams, and press the seams open.

2 Fold back 1.5cm (½in) at one short end of one of the two strips, and machine stitch 8mm (¼in) from the folded edge. Then turn under 1.5cm (½in) all along the lower edge of the strip, and press, using a short clear plastic ruler to check the width. Using matching thread, machine stitch along the lower edge 8mm (¼in) from the folded edge. Press to embed the stitches.

3 Fold up the strip and send or take it to a commercial pleater for

The permanently-pleated frill is the ultimate in elegance, especially when made with 4mm (⅛in) pleats (as seen above). The pleating is done professionally by commercial pleaters.

pleating, specifying the width of pleat desired.

4 The fabric will return pleated and lightly stuck to a very thin paper. Unroll the frill, and, using paper-cutting scissors, cut roughly around the strip(s) without pulling off the paper. Machine stitch along the top of the frill 1cm (⅜in) from the raw edge, stitching through both fabric and paper. This will hold the top of the pleats in place.

5 Before setting the frill into the pelmet, as for steps 5 and 6 of the machine-gathered frill, gently tear away the thin paper.

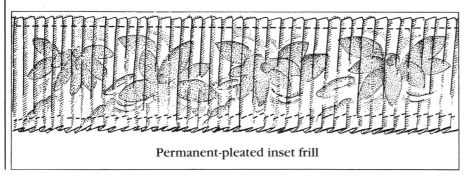

Permanent-pleated inset frill

Chapter Three

BEFORE YOU BEGIN

The decision to make your own window treatments is a highly admirable one. You have made this decision because you are a creative person with an aptitude for sewing. But before you begin it is essential that you set yourself up correctly with certain basic equipment. In this chapter I list and explain these basic tools. I then go on to explain in detail how to make the simple calculations for curtain material quantities and how to set up your pelmet board and curtain rod.

BASIC EQUIPMENT

Having the correct tools will turn the whole job of curtain making into an easy task, allowing you to work fast and efficiently. Although a professional curtain maker may have a larger work space and larger tables to work on, the tools that he or she uses are the same as those listed below.

You will see that the equipment requirements listed below are minimal. Aside from the obvious sewing machine and iron, they include: two pairs of curtain maker's table clamps, a large trestle table, a 2m (6ft) folding ruler, a 15cm (6in) transparent plastic ruler, a soft tape measure, sewing scissors and pinking shears, a pocket calculator, a manual staple gun (for pelmets), an aluminium stepladder, and extra-long pins and needles.

Curtain maker's table clamps
Two pairs of extra-strong table clamps (see below) are probably more important than any of the other tools listed. They enable you to deal with huge amounts of material on a relatively small table.

What the clamps do is hold the material very firmly in place, never

Trestle table

allowing it to move while you are cutting, sewing or pinning long lengths of fabric. They also enable you to manoeuvre into place interlining, lining or fusible buckram while your curtain fabric remains still. The difference between sewing stretched and clamped fabric and loose fabric is extraordinary. The clamps will make the sewing both quicker and easier, and the hand stitches will automatically become more regular and even in tension. For me, using clamps is like having another person always helping you – but silently!

The type of clamp pictured has no jagged edges and will never mark your chintz in any way, nor will it damage any ordinary hardwood table. However, it is not advisable to risk using any sort of clamp on a valuable antique table.

Although these clamps are not always easy to find, they are well worth the search. Professional photographic equipment shops sometimes stock them. (Also see the list of suppliers on page 128.)

Trestle table
You must never try to work on the floor. It is both uncomfortable and impractical. Physically it is terribly bad for your back and your circulation. In addition, working on the floor does not allow the use of the invaluable table clamps.

A sturdy trestle table measuring approximately 1.80m by 70cm (6ft

by 2ft 3in) is the minimum-sized table you could successfully work on when sewing fairly wide curtain panels, such as a finished flat width of 3m (9ft 10in). Obviously, however, the bigger the table is, the better it is for you. The table must also have a wide enough lip, which is not too thick, to accommodate the table clamps.

As already mentioned it is not advisable to use an antique table for curtain making. Aside from being marked by clamps, it could be scratched by the needle when interlocking the interlining to the curtain.

You must always sit while you work. If you stand you will end up bending over your work, which is a strain on your back. Simply move your chair around the table to the side you are working on at the time.

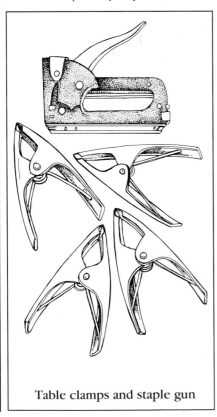
Table clamps and staple gun

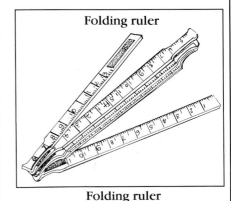
Folding ruler

Folding ruler
A wooden folding ruler 2m (6ft) long is an absolute necessity for curtain making. A ruler with metric

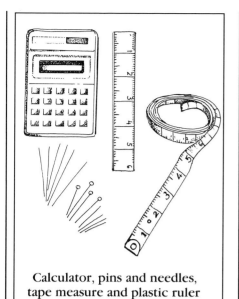

Calculator, pins and needles, tape measure and plastic ruler

measurements on one side and inches and feet on the other is especially useful for those who are just getting to grips with the metric system. (Remember, though, to choose one system and *stick to it*; trying to mix the two is a recipe for disaster.) This type of ruler is brilliant, as it enables you to measure any curtain drop up to 4m (13ft) without having to use a ladder. This is because it is totally rigid, like a yardstick, and can easily be held up the side of a window architrave to measure it (see *Measuring the drop* on page 33).

A long folding ruler is also used when measuring the drop of a curtain from the finished hem upwards to determine how much material to fold back along the top. Using a rigid measuring instrument for this purpose is much easier and quicker than using a soft tape measure.

Transparent plastic ruler
A transparent plastic ruler 15cm (6in) long is a very efficient little item to use for measuring while sewing, and is often more practical than a soft tape measure. Being small and flat, it rarely slips onto the foor, unlike a tape measure. Also, you can see through it, as you gently turn back hems to their correct width. Especially on an ironing board, a little ruler is the only thing to use if you want to work fast and efficiently.

Soft tape measure
I rarely use a soft tape measure. But there are two situations when it must be substituted for your long rigid ruler. The first instance is when you need to measure around the girth of a curtain to estimate the size of the tie-back. The other instance is when measuring the width of a curved bay window.

Scissors and pinking shears
It may be obvious that you must always use a very good pair of large sewing scissors to make cutting-out easier, but I feel that this point is worth reiterating. Bad scissors are frustrating and will slow you down considerably – for example when you are trying to cut interlining away from the corners of your curtains.

Good scissors are not expensive, but it is essential to hide them from the rest of the family so that they are used for cutting material and nothing else. Paper will blunt them immediately.

Pinking shears are needed for edges that will be turned to the wrong side but not doubled under, such as on certain handmade frills (see page 20).

Pocket calculator
There is no point in doing multiplication and division yourself, when a calculator will do it for you in a fraction of a second. This small piece of equipment makes calculating fabric quantities, pattern repeats, and sizes and positions of French pleats quick and painless.

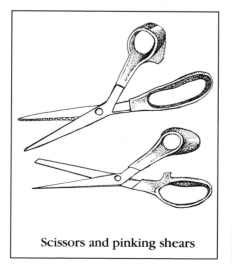

Scissors and pinking shears

Stepladder

Staple gun
You can buy a manual staple gun in any do-it-yourself shop, and you will find it invaluable. This is primarily because the only way to put up any pelmet (with the exception of a certain section of a swag and tail, see step 2 on page 100) is with Velcro. One side of the Velcro, the 'hard' side, is stapled onto the front of the pelmet board, which is fixed to the wall above the window. The other, 'soft', side is sewn onto the back of the top of the pelmet. I also always use Velcro when hanging Austrian or Roman blinds.

Stepladder
An average-sized aluminium step-ladder will be tall enough if the top of your window is up to 3m (10ft) from the floor. A window taller than this will require a larger ladder. Although a wooden ladder will do, I much prefer an aluminium one because it is so light and easy to move around.

Extra-long pins and needles
Pins and needles may be a normal part of sewing equipment, but for curtain making it is important to use

extra-long pins and needles. Extra-long pins with round glass or plastic ends are particularly useful when working on curtains.

The type of needles required for the long stitches used in curtain making are *long darners*. You will waste a lot of time and effort trying to use shorter needles or pins.

MEASURING THE WINDOW

Apart from certain special windows with distinctive architectural features, like Gothic or Georgian windows, the average window is not, to me, a very exciting object in aesthetic terms. Therefore, there is every reason in the world to dress it up and give it a marvellous creative treatment. The main reasons for curtaining a window are:

– To soften the lines of the window
– To control the amount of light
– To insulate the room
– To create something of beauty

To fulfil all of these requirements successfully it is of the utmost importance to measure the window with great accuracy, so that the curtain design will be perfectly balanced.

Curtain lengths

Always remember that the longer you can make a pelmet or curtain design for a particular room, the more elegant the window treatment will look – in other words, LENGTH IS ELEGANCE.

The methods described in *Measuring the drop* (page 33) allow for the drop of the curtain to just touch the carpet but no more. This is the length that I would almost always recommend. The few exceptions usually occur where there is an obstruction under the window, as there is for a window above a sink, for example.

Disadvantages of extra-long curtains

In some instances adding an extra 15cm (6in) onto full-length curtains can look very lavish and full. But there are four great disadvantages to these extra-long curtains: the curtains do not hang as well as when they just come to the floor; you have to take trouble to dress, or

Floor-length and extra-long curtains

arrange, them every day; pets come and lie on them; and it is hard to run the vacuum around them. So it is as well to keep these disadvantages in mind before embarking on making extra-long curtains (see illustration above).

Drop for curtains with pelmets

Measuring the 'drop' or length of your curtains is the first thing you need to do when determining the amount of curtain material you will need. If you are using a pelmet to crown your curtains, the curtains will begin at the underside of the *pelmet board*. This is a flat piece of wood which juts out into the room from the wall. It holds the curtain rod, and the pelmet is hung from its edge (see page 39 for illustration of pelmet board with rod).

Pelmet positions

To determine the drop of your curtains, you must first decide on the position of the board. If the board is already in place, and you are happy with its position, then you can measure from this board. But make sure that the board is *securely fastened to the wall* (see page 39).

The obvious place for the pelmet board is sitting horizontally on the top of the window architrave (or frame). However, if you want to create height you can position the board higher above the architrave, thus gaining as much extra height as you like. The space between the top of the architrave and the bottom of the pelmet board is called 'dead wall', since it is the wall that will eventually be permanently hidden behind the pelmet. By raising the pelmet board above the window frame you will have 'raised' the height of the window and made it look taller and narrower than it actually is. Visually you are 'raising' the height of the ceiling.

There are three possible reasons for wanting to do this:

– To enable you to create a deep pelmet
  To minimize loss of light
– To make a low ceiling appear higher

You may wish to create the deepest pelmet possible, while retaining the balance between curtain and pelmet, and between window treatment and room, with a view to maximum elegance. Minimizing the loss of light through the window is also a consideration to keep in mind, especially if the window is north- or east-facing and if the function of the room requires maximum light. Lastly, 'raising' a low ceiling will help to create the illusion of more space in your room.

Once you have decided on the position of your pelmet board, you should make sure that you will be able to fix the correct size of board to the wall in this position. Read the section on *Pelmet boards* (page 39).

Measuring the drop

1 Only after the position of your pelmet board has been decided can

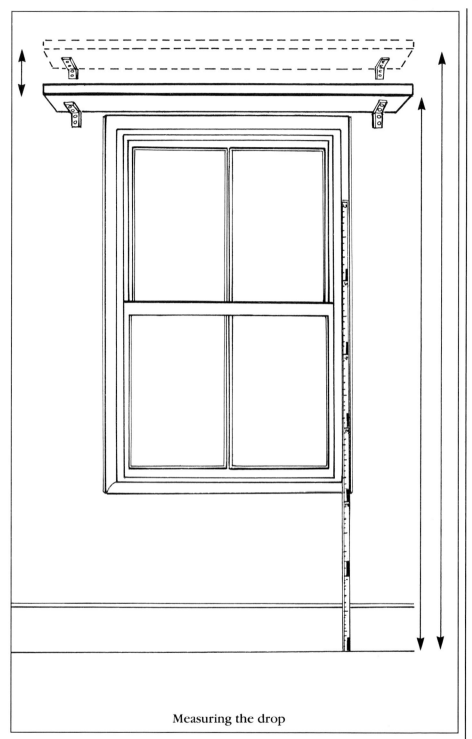

Measuring the drop

you begin to measure the curtain drop. Unfold your long folding ruler and hold it fully extended up against the architrave, or window frame, at one side of the window, with the end of the ruler which is marked with 2m (6ft) resting on the floor. Make a faint mark with a soft pencil on the window frame at the top of the ruler. (See illustration of measuring the drop above.)

2 Then move the extended ruler up until the top of it just reaches the point where the bottom of the pelmet board will be, either at the top of the architrave or a short distance above it as desired. '

3 Add together the 2 measurements just obtained to determine the total measurement between the floor and the bottom of the pelmet board. To

determine the curtain drop from this figure you must subtract 3cm (1⅛in) – of which 2cm (¾in) is for the drop of the curtain rod and its runners and 1cm (⅜in) is for the unlaid carpet (assuming the carpet has a shallow pile). If the carpet is already in place, subtract only the 2cm (¾in) to accommodate the curtain rod and runners. If the pelmet board is being placed up against the ceiling and you have measured up to the ceiling, remove a further 2cm (¾in) to allow for the thickness of the pelmet board (see *Size of pelmet board* on page 39 for board measurements).

Drop of curtains without pelmets

I stress the use of pelmets in your window treatments because of the elegance and versatility of pelmet designs. But there are instances where window treatments should be designed without pelmets and can instead be treated in other ways, such as hung from poles. Measuring the drop for curtains without pelmets is dealt with in detail in Chapter 5.

Window clearance

The next step in measuring your window, after the curtain drop has been calculated, is to measure the window width. But before beginning to measure the window width, always check for anything that will obstruct the clearance around the window. Obstructions that can cause a problem are:

– A boxed-in radiator
– An adjacent wall
– The door of an adjacent cupboard (or closet)
– A ceiling beam

You must take these obstructions into consideration and adjust your width measurements accordingly. Whatever happens, the whole curtain and pelmet design must be one hundred per cent symmetrical with the window itself. Otherwise the curtains will draw together off-centre. Also, the pelmet board must be absolutely level (not necessarily with the top of the window). This can be determined with the aid of a spirit level.

TABLE 1
Approximate Number of Curtain Widths and Housing Space Required for a Window

The number of curtain widths** given here is approximate and is based on a 137cm (54in)-wide curtain material, which is interlined with a medium-weight interlining.

Note: This guide is for a quick reference only and TABLE 4 should be read before purchasing fabric.

Window width*	No. of widths** in each curtain	Housing space each side of window
50cm (1ft 8in)	½ width	5cm (2in)
80cm (2ft 7in)	1 width	7cm (2¾in)
1.25m (4ft 1in)	1½ widths	10cm (4in)
1.60m (5ft 3in)	2 widths	15cm (6in)
1.90m (6ft 3in)	2 widths	15cm (6in)
2.40m (7ft 11in)	2½ widths	20cm (8in)
2.80m (9ft 2½in)	3 widths	25cm (10in)
3.30m (10ft 10in)	3½ widths	30cm (12in)
3.80m (12ft 6in)	4 widths	30cm (12in)

* Window width is measured from edge of architrave to edge of architrave.

Measuring window width

The window width is measured from edge to edge of the vertical parts of the architrave, or window frame, on either side of the window. Determining the width of the window is the first step in determining both the width of the pelmet board and the width of each finished flat curtain.

Curtain-housing space

To accommodate, or 'house', the curtains when they are drawn fully open, a certain amount of wall space on either side of the window needs to be available (see *Window clearance*). The curtains must hang clear of the window when they are open, so that they do not reduce any of the light coming into the room. Nor will they get too dirty, as might happen if they were hung in front of a French window.

Table 1 (above) indicates approximately how much empty wall space will be needed on either side of the window (outside the architrave) to house the curtains on different window widths. The housing space (U.S. 'stackback') given for each window width will be the approximate amount necessary to clear the curtains off the window.

Thus to determine the size of the pelmet board, add the width of the window and that of the housing space on either side of the window (see page 39).

Curtain material widths

Table 1 also gives the approximate number of widths (selvedge to selvedge) of curtain material that should be used for each curtain for a given window width. This table is for quick reference only. It is based on a 137cm (54in)-wide fabric which is interlined with a medium-weight interlining. Although furnishing fabrics come in both wider and narrower widths, this width is one of the most common.

If you are using material of a different width, you can follow a very simple rule to calculate the width of your finished curtain. The general rule that **Table 1** follows is that each finished curtain, when flat, should measure not less than 2⅓ times the width it must cover (including the housing space and

To achieve perfect balance and symmetry in your window treatment you have to measure your window accurately, allowing equal housing space on each side (as seen right).

TABLE 2
Determining Width of Pelmet Board for Sample Window

This is an example of how to calculate the width of your pelmet board.

First measure:

Window width	1.25m	(4ft 1in)
(architrave to architrave)		

Then determine *housing space* by referring to TABLE 1 (page 34):

Total housing space	10cm (4in) × 2 = 20cm (8in)	
(on both sides of window)		

To determine the pelmet board width simply add the *window width* and the *total housing space*:

Window width	1.25m	(4ft 1in)
Total housing space	+ 20cm	(8in)
Pelmet board width	**1.45m**	**(4ft 9in)**

---

the extra width allowance – see **Table 2** above) and not more than 2½ times the width.

When deciding how many material widths you need, do not cut widths less than one-half the width of the material. The difference a narrower width makes is not worth the effort, so if in doubt always go for a slightly wider curtain. Remember that 2½ times the width is an *approximate* aim.

One exception to the fullness suggested is for a very narrow window – such as the 50cm (1ft 8in)-wide window – where you may not want so much fullness. This is especially true where a small window requires a quite shallow pelmet board which could not accommodate such a full curtain.

The other exception is when you want your curtains to look especially full and lavish. In this case, you can add an extra half width onto each curtain panel listed in the table, but do not necessarily adjust your housing space. Generally, however, a finished interlined curtain 2½ times the width it needs to cover, will be quite full enough.

The next section describes in detail how to calculate the width each finished pleated curtain must cover once it is hanging.

DETERMINING FABRIC AMOUNTS

Once you have calculated the curtain drop that you require and measured the width of your window from one outer edge of the architrave to the other, you can begin the process of determining

the amount of curtain material that you will need for your particular curtain design.

Curtain and pelmet-board widths
Tables 2 and **3** (above and below) give an example of how you should make your calculations. They establish a hypothetical or sample window and show clearly how to work out the pelmet-board width and the finished curtain width.

The treatment for this window includes a pelmet, but the principles for the calculations are the same for other types of curtain design. The exception is that for curtains hanging from poles, for instance, the drop is measured from the pole (see page 62).

Pelmet-board width
As you can see from **Table 2**, the pelmet-board width is determined by adding the housing space required (see **Table 1**) to the window width measured between the outer edges of the architrave.

Extra width allowance
For curtains with a pelmet you must add an extra 10cm (4in) to each curtain to accommodate the overlap arm (U.S. 'master slide') on the curtain rod and the fact that the

---

TABLE 3
Determining Finished Width
of each Sample Curtain Heading after Pleating

This is an example of how to determine the *finished width* of each of the two curtains across the heading after pleating.

First calculate the measurement of *one half of the pelmet board width* (see TABLE 2):

Pelmet board width	1.45m	(4ft 9in)
1.45m (4ft 9in) ÷ 2 =	72.5cm	(2ft 4½in)
One half of pelmet board width	**72.5cm**	**(2ft 4½in)**

Then add ½ the *pelmet board width* and the *extra width allowance* (for the overlap arm at the centre of the rod and for the pelmet board return):

One half of pelmet board width	72.5cm	(2ft 4½in)
Extra width allowance	+ 10cm	(4in)
Finished width of curtain after pleating	**82.5cm**	**(2ft 8½in)**

---

curtains turn into the wall at the sides. The ends of the pelmet board are called the 'pelmet-board returns'.

It is essential that the ends of your curtains do meet the wall at the sides, because a gap looks very unappealing and because you want to stop all draughts coming from the window (see screw eye on pelmet board page 40).

The extra width allowance of 10cm (4in) is calculated on the basis of a rod that has a 5cm (2in) overlap at the centre and a pelmet-board 17cm (6¾in) deep (see *Pelmet board* page 39).

Finished width of pleated curtain
Of course, each curtain will have to extend across half of the pelmet board once it has been pleated. But the *extra width allowance* must also be added to each curtain to cover the overlap arm and the curtain turning into the wall – called the 'return'.

When you are gathering your curtain up on the special heading tape or pleating your curtain, this total width of each finished pleated curtain is the width you are aiming for (see **Table 3** left).

This is also the width that you must multiply by 2½ to estimate how wide the finished flat curtain must be (see *Curtain material widths* page 34).

Calculating the amount of fabric
Table 4 (right) illustrates how to calculate the required material for the sample window in **Table 2**. After you have determined the necessary curtain drop as well as the number of fabric widths needed for each curtain, you are ready to calculate the amount of curtain material you will need to purchase.

This calculation is, of course, a very important one, as a mistake can be very expensive. So do not rush the process. Take as much time as you need, first to measure your windows and then to make calculations. Check your calculations (and measurements, for that matter) at least twice.

If you have a friend who has experience with curtain making, you may want her or him to check the

---

TABLE 4
Calculating Curtain Material Needed for Sample Window

This is an example of how to calculate the quantity of material needed for the curtains for the sample window in TABLE 2 (not including the pelmet fabric). The hypothetical curtain material has a pattern repeat of 33cm (13in), and the curtains will have a *pencil-pleat* (U.S. 'shirred') *heading*.

Note: The *turn-down** allowance at the top of the curtain is determined by the type of heading chosen.

First calculate the unsewn drop or 'cutting length' of each width by adding curtain drop, hem and turn-down at top:

1) Curtain Drop	2.80m	(9ft	2½in)
2) Hem at bottom of curtain	12cm		(4¾in)
3) Turn-down* at top	10cm		(4in)
Cutting length	3.02m	(9ft	11¼in)

Now add the length of the pattern repeat to calculate the drop allowance needed:

1) Cutting length	3.02m	(9ft	11¼in)
2) Pattern repeat	33cm		(13in)
Each drop allowance measures	3.35m	(11ft	¼in)

Then decide how many widths you need altogether for both curtains (see TABLE 1) and multiply this by the *drop allowance*:

Drop allowance	3.35m	(11ft ¼in)
No. of widths = 3		
(1½ widths for each curtain)	× 3	
	10.05m	(33ft ¾in)

You will need to purchase .... **10m (11yd) of material**

---

calculations for you. A fresh eye may sometimes catch a simple but important oversight. The sales assistants where you purchase your material usually have a good deal of knowledge of curtain making, and because you are making such a big purchase, they should be willing to check your fabric estimate.

Extra drop allowances
As you can see from **Table 4**, to calculate the total length to allow for each unsewn drop of curtain material you must add allowances for the following:

– Hem at bottom of curtain
– Turn-down at top of curtain
– Pattern repeat

Generally 12cm (4¾in) is the measurement for hemming on all

lined curtains. The turn-down at the top of the curtain will vary according to the type of heading you have chosen. The sample curtain has a turn-down allowance at the top of 10cm (4in) which is enough for a pencil pleat (U.S. 'shirred') heading.

The excess amount allowed for the pattern repeat also varies from one material to another. A totally plain fabric, of course, will not need an allowance added for pattern repeats. But for all printed materials and even for some textured patterns, you should always measure the length of each pattern repeat.

Pattern matching is not difficult so long as you have allowed sufficient excess for each drop. You will need to add on one pattern repeat for every drop of material (see **Table 4** above for an example of how to add on the pattern repeat allowance).

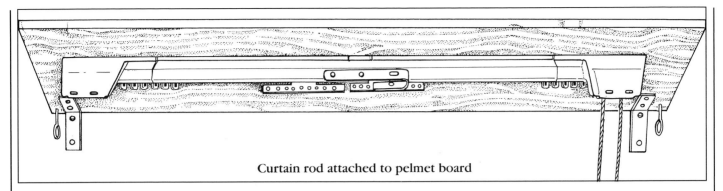

Curtain rod attached to pelmet board

Lining and interlining amounts

The lining and interlining are always the same width as the curtains. But because there is no need for pattern matching, you will probably need less material.

You must take into account the width from selvedge to selvedge of the lining and interlining. This may not match the width of the curtain material. Whatever the fabric width, the joined widths must cover the same distance as the joined curtain material widths.

Pelmet material amounts

If you are making a pelmet, you should add the amount for your pelmet into your total calculation for material. The instructions for calculating this are given in Chapter 6 (page 71)

It may not be necessary to add on for *trimmings* (see pages 20–28), as you may have enough material left over from the excess added for pattern repeats. However, do calculate carefully the total amount needed for frills.

FIXING PELMET BOARD AND RODS

Making and fixing a pelmet board and curtain rod is not, of course, a skill one would expect a curtain maker to have. The instructions are given here in detail because they are an important part of achieving a successful curtain design. It is, however, advisable to get someone with experience to do the carpentry.

In some cases, in order to obtain the longest possible length for your curtains, you will have to place the pelmet board as close as possible to the ceiling (as seen left).

Especially when attaching the pelmet board to the wall, not hiring a professional is a false economy. The pelmet board needs to be strong enough to hold the weight of great lengths of lined and interlined material. It may not be apparent to an amateur how to fix the pelmet successfully to the wall above the window, and damage can inadvertently be done to the wall.

Size of pelmet board

The pelmet board should almost always be 17cm (6¾in) deep and 2cm (¾in) thick. The curtain rail is fixed lengthwise to the centre of the board, ending about 2cm (¾in) from each end.

When purchasing the board at a timber yard, you should ask for '7in by 1in' board. If you actually measure it you will find it is closer to 6¾in by ¾in. This is because once a '7 by 1' has been planed it is no longer quite as wide or as thick as its name implies.

I only use a narrower board where the room and window treatment are quite small and where I therefore would not want a deep pelmet board jutting out into the room – it would look too cumbersome and heavy. In this case a board no narrower than 10cm to 12.5cm (4in to 5in) would be used.

The width of the board is determined by the width of the window treatment. It should extend past the window the width required for the housing space on either side (see **Table 2** on page 36).

Fascia and vertical returns

If you are hanging a pelmet that has a fusible buckram band at its top (see page 76), you will need a strong plywood fascia along the front of the board for support and vertical timber returns. (In American terminology you will need a 'cornice board'.) The plywood fascia is fixed to the front of the standard-sized pelmet board, and the vertical timber returns (or sides) must be screwed into the ends of the board (see below). The buckram-faced pelmet is stretched across the fascia and around the sharp corners.

The vertical returns should be made in the same '7 by 1' timber as the pelmet board and will therefore measure 17cm (6¾in) square and 2cm (¾in) thick.

The fascia should be made of 3mm (⅛in)-thick strong plywood. If the pelmet will have a fusible buckram band at its top, cut the plywood so that it is just slightly longer, vertically, than the buckram. For example, if the band is 12cm (4¾in) deep, use a plywood fascia about 14cm (5½in) deep.

Curtain rods

A good-quality curtain rod with a pulley system (in American termi-

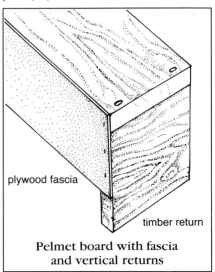

Pelmet board with fascia and vertical returns

nology a 'traverse rod') is essential (see page 128 for where to purchase rods). The curtains will be opened and closed countless times, and a good rod and pulley system will work smoothly for a long time.

Rods come in various types. You can get ones that are 'telescopic', which pull and push to differing sizes. Good curtain-rod manufacturers will also make made-to-measure rods, heavy-duty or regular, made to your own specifications. They will even make special rods to curve around a bay window if necessary.

Look for rods that have very clear instructions for attaching them. When using a pelmet board, you will want a rod that has a 'top fix' so that it can be screwed to the board above it. A good metal rod will have clear instructions on how to load and unload the runners and centralize the overlap arm.

Attaching the curtain rod

With very rare exceptions, the rod must be attached to the pelmet board rather than to the wall. Timber is far stronger and more reliable than plaster. Once the rod is on the board, the board is screwed firmly to the wall. The weight of the curtains will then be evenly distributed along the rod. More importantly, the stress of the pully system, at one end of the rail, will be well accommodated in the timber and not at one pressure point in the plaster. Remember that plaster is unreliable, especially in a very old house.

The rod should be set halfway back from the front of the board (see page 39). This is essential so that full curtains, as they are drawn backwards and forwards, will not in any way disturb beautifully dressed pelmets. Hence the necessity of pelmet boards 17cm (6¾in) wide and no less!

Brackets and screws

The brackets are attached to the pelmet board at either end (see page 39). A central bracket is advisable if the board is over about 1.40m (4½ft).

Use very tough, strong brackets about 5cm by 8cm (2in by 3in).

Securely attach each bracket into the timber board with 2 screws.

Screw eyes on pelmet board

Because you are top-fixing the rod and not using the wall brackets provided with the rod, you do lose one advantage; this is the use of the special holes in the wall brackets, which would enable you to turn a right angle with your curtain to meet the wall. Instead, you have to create your own system for the curtain to reach the wall. This is easily done. Merely place a large screw eye, about 3cm (1¼in) long at both back corners of the board (see illustration below).

The last curtain hook is hooked into this screw eye, thereby turning the end of the curtain into the wall.

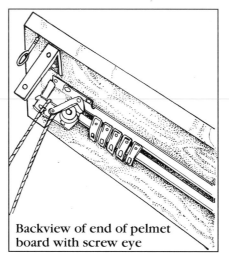

Backview of end of pelmet board with screw eye

Fixing pelmet board to wall

The screws that attach each bracket to the wall should be at least 3cm (1¼in) long. Rawl plugs need to be inserted into the holes in the wall, and the pelmet board should be fixed in a level position using a spirit level. It is highly recommended that you hire a professional to attach your pelmet board. It is not worth risking damaging your wall or having your curtains fall down.

The pulley system

You must, if you possibly can, employ a pulley system. One of the few situations in which you cannot is when you are using wooden poles (see page 62). Pulley systems give the curtains every chance of success. It is essential that your hands,

however clean, do not yank the curtains twice a day. The leading edges at the centre will get dirty, and the dirt, along with the effects of the sun, will eventually cause the fabric to rot.

I once visited a wonderful house in the Eastern Highlands of Zimbabwe where the servants still employed the old-fashioned method of putting on white gloves before hand-pulling the curtains. Perhaps you cannot buy good curtain rails with pulley systems in Zimbabwe!

Types of pulley systems

There are two choices you have for a pulley system. One choice is to use the plastic tensioner in the curtain-rod kit. It is screwed into the skirting board (U.S. 'baseboard') near the floor or into the wall. The continuous nylon cord is looped onto the sprung tensioner. The cord is then shortened from the centre at the overlap arm (see overlap arm on rod on page 39) until it is tight.

Complete instructions for setting up the system are provided with the curtain rod.

The second choice you have for your pulley system is the one I prefer. I use a pair of brass acorns in place of the plastic tensioner.

First you should follow the curtain-rod instructions to centralize the overlap arm.

You then cut the cord to the desired length and thread the two cord ends through a tiny S-hook 1.5cm (½in) long to prevent them from twisting. After this, thread each end through a brass acorn.

However, if your window is very wide and not very tall – for example, 3.50m (11½ft) wide and 2.15m (7ft) tall – then you have to use the plastic tensioner. This will allow the continuous cord, within the rod, to draw the curtains backwards and forwards. If you were to cut the cord to put brass acorns on, you could not draw the curtains backwards and forwards without having a large length of cord lying on the floor.

Chapter Four

MAKING A START

Having taken the window measurements and calculated the quantity of curtain
material that you will need, you are finally ready to begin making your curtains.
For this you will need only the most basic sewing techniques. This chapter contains
step-by-step instructions for making simple interlined curtains with a pencil-pleat
heading – the most suitable heading for all curtains with a pelmet (see example of
pencil pleats above). I lay out for you all of my professional tips in how to deal with
large quantities of material and how to successfully line and interline curtains.

CUTTING FABRICS

Having purchased your curtain material, lining and interlining (see page 36), you can now proceed to create your window treatment. Making your pelmets will come last.

To prepare for cutting your fabrics, pull your work table out into the room so that you can easily walk around it. Make sure that the floor is very clean around the table, as the lengths of fabric will often need to hang onto the floor. And lastly, have all the necessary tools close to hand.

The sample curtains

To take you as clearly as possible through the step-by-step process of making a pair of simple lined and interlined pencil-pleated curtains, I will use the sample curtains introduced in Chapter 2 as the example in the instructions. In this way, I will be able to use specific measurements when explaining the techniques – which should help you to visualize the process.

The dimensions of the sample curtains are the same ones used in Chapter 2 in **Tables 1**, **2** and **3** and are as follows:

– Finished drop 2.80m (9ft 2½in)
– Cutting length 3.02m (9ft 11¼in)
– 1½ widths for each curtain

The pencil-pleat heading has been chosen for the sample curtains because it is the heading that is both the simplest to make and the best heading for curtains with a pelmet (see various *Heading tapes* on pages 51–52).

The cutting length

The cutting length for each width of curtain material is always determined by adding to the desired finished curtain drop the allowance for the hem at the bottom and the turn-down at the top (see **Table 4** on page 37).

In the case of our sample curtains we are adding 10cm (4in) for the turn-down at the top of the curtain, which is sufficient for a pencil-pleat heading. The turn-down is not the same for every type of heading, so make sure you know exactly what is required for the type of heading you have chosen.

For instance, if you are making French or goblet pleats at the top of your curtain, you will have to add on 18cm (7in) for the turn-down instead of only 10cm (4in). The reason for this is that for these types of pleat the material is folded to the wrong side over the lining and must cover the whole length of the fusible buckram (see page 52), which may be as deep as 15cm (6in). The excess below the depth of the buckram is then turned under again so that no raw edge is exposed. (See page 56 for French-pleated curtains and page 60 for goblet-pleated curtains).

Cutting the curtain material

1 Check your calculations one last time to make sure that the *cutting length* of each width of material is correct, and check that you have enough fabric.

2 Before measuring the first width, or 'drop', check that the grain of the material is straight along the starting edge. To do this, unfold the material so that the starting edge is aligned with one end of the table and one selvedge aligned with the edge of the length of the table. With the selvedge aligned with the table in this way you can use the right-angle corner at the end of the table to straighten the end of the material.

Clamp the material to the table before cutting to hold it in place (see *Table clamps* page 30). Then, resting the scissors along the edge of the table as you cut, trim the top of the material to straighten it.

3 With the starting edge still level with one end of the table, unroll the material the whole length of the table and clamp it in place, keeping one selvedge aligned with the edge of the table. Using the unfolded 2m (6ft) folding ruler, measure down along the selvedge as far as your table will allow and, with a pencil, mark the selvedge. Then unclamp and unroll more material, moving it onto the table. Again measure down along the selvedge until the total cutting length is reached, and mark the selvedge. Unclamp, move back to the beginning of the material and measure down the other selvedge in the same way.

4 In order to mark the cutting line, gently turn the material 90 degrees, so that the selvedges are running perpendicular to the length of the table and both selvedges are resting on it. Put your long ruler across the table and join up the two final marks on the selvedges. Draw a line across the material, running the pencil along the ruler. (If you are worried

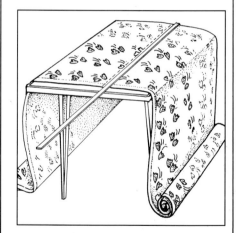

about marking the material you can use a disappearing marker or pins – but if you have carefully checked your cutting length calculations and fabric amount, you will not be running any risk.) Cut along the line using straight-edged scissors.

5 You must now cut the remaining widths – for the sample curtains 3 widths are required (1½ for each curtain). Unroll another quantity of material and clamp in the same way as for the first width. Take the first width you have already cut, and match its pattern with the uncut

material (see diagram below of pattern-matching). Make a mark on the selvedge to indicate where the next length of fabric will begin. Measure the distance from the mark just made to the top of the material, so that you can now mark the opposite selvedge the same distance from the top. Join up the two marks as you did for the lower edge of the first width. Now cut along this line.

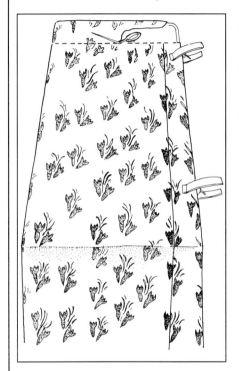

This removes any excess of the pattern repeat, so that the pattern will match at the seams. You are now ready to cut the second width. Repeat the same process followed when cutting the first width. Cut as many widths as required in the same way, pattern-matching each width.

6 After all of the necessary widths of curtain material have been cut, they should be stored with care while the lining and interlining widths are cut. First cut any half widths needed by cutting a single width in half lengthwise. Roll the widths you will not be using right away back onto the bolt to avoid creasing them. This is not easy, and if possible you should get the help of another person, who can guide the widths of material back onto the bolt as you turn it. They may spiral off a little at one end, but do not worry. So long as the widths are rolled up in this

manner they will never crease. Creases, especially in chintz, are very hard to get rid of without the use of a steam iron. (Always iron the material from the wrong side, since the steam would damage the glaze of the chintz.)

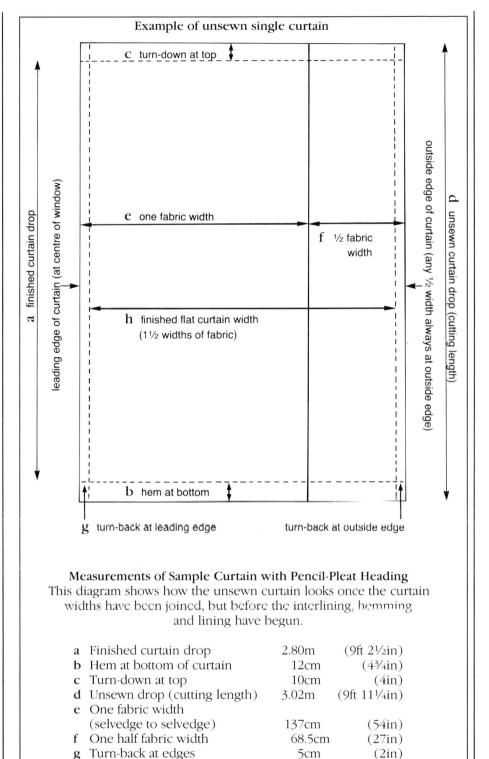

Example of unsewn single curtain

Measurements of Sample Curtain with Pencil-Pleat Heading
This diagram shows how the unsewn curtain looks once the curtain widths have been joined, but before the interlining, hemming and lining have begun.

a	Finished curtain drop	2.80m	(9ft 2½in)
b	Hem at bottom of curtain	12cm	(4¾in)
c	Turn-down at top	10cm	(4in)
d	Unsewn drop (cutting length)	3.02m	(9ft 11¼in)
e	One fabric width (selvedge to selvedge)	137cm	(54in)
f	One half fabric width	68.5cm	(27in)
g	Turn-back at edges	5cm	(2in)
h	Approximate finished flat curtain width	1.94m	(6ft 4in)

Cutting lining and interlining
For the lining and the interlining you will need exactly the same width across the curtain, but they can be cut slightly shorter. This is because the lining and the interlining will eventually be

trimmed to end at the top of the final curtain drop.

To determine the cutting length for the lining and the interlining of pencil-pleated curtains, subtract 8cm (3in) from the curtain-material cutting length. For French or goblet pleating, the lining and interlining are cut 14cm (5½in) shorter than the curtain-material widths.

Follow the instructions for cutting the curtain material, when cutting the lining and interlining, but use the slightly shorter cutting length for each width and omit the pattern-matching.

After cutting, fold up the lining and interlining and set them aside until you are ready to use them.

JOINING THE WIDTHS
Once all of your fabric pieces have been cut, you can machine stitch the widths together. The lining and interlining will need to be joined to make up the same width as the curtain width.

Remember, whole widths must be placed nearest the centre of the window, and any half width on the outside. The diagram on page 43 shows the sample curtain once the widths have been joined and before it has been interlined and lined.

Curtain-material selvedges
Selvedges are rarely cut off on any curtain material. On some fabrics, however, there may be a situation when the writing on the selvedge is rather prominent. And if the background of the print is white, then it is important that the writing not show through, so it has to be cut off. The selvedge may also cause a problem if it is rather tight, which sometimes happens with linen. In this case it is sufficient to snip the selvedge intermittently to ease it.

Joining curtain-material widths
Before machine stitching the curtain-material widths together, you must pin the seam edges together. If the fabric is plain and does not require pattern-matching, you can simply place the edges together with right sides facing, pin and machine stitch. If your material is a print, however, it must be pattern-matched while pinning.

Pattern-joining curtain material
1 Clamp the first width of curtain material to the table, right side up, with the selvedge running along the very edge of the length of the table and the top of the curtain at one end. (Remember, you will be joining half widths to the outside edge of each curtain.)

2 Now take the second width or, as in the case of our sample curtain, half width, and line up the selvedge of the second width (also right side up) with the first width on the table so that the pattern matches. Turn under the selvedge of the second width, and pin it to the clamped

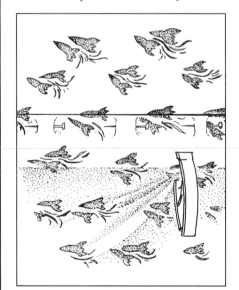

width, matching the pattern carefully. Pin the two pieces together along the length of the table, inserting the pins vertically along the turned-under selvedge and placing them about 21cm (8in) apart.

3 Before moving the fabric along to pin the rest of the seam, run the closed blades of your scissors along the pinned seam. By doing this you will make a permanent, firm crease along the fold line. This is a quick and effective way of making a crease without using a hot iron. The reason for the hard crease will become apparent in a moment. Unclamp the material, then pin and crease the rest of the seam in the same way.

4 Then, beginning at the top of the curtain again, bring the second

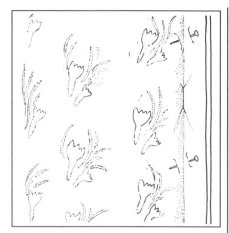

width over on top of the first width, so that the right sides of the pieces are together. Now insert a pin horizontally across the sharp fold line made in step 3, in each space between the vertical pins (see above). Do this along the entire length of the curtain.

5 After all of the horizontal pins are in place, remove the first lot of vertical pins.

6 You are now ready to machine stitch the two widths accurately down the sharp fold line. Any additional widths are pinned and sewn in the same way, with any half width always placed at the outside edge of the curtain.

Machine stitching curtain widths
Before seaming the curtain material, test your machine on a scrap of the fabric. If there is a problem, continue experimenting on remnants of the material until the tension and size of your stitches (fairly large) are correct. This is much more satisfactory than having to unpick errors in the actual curtain.

Always use matching thread and a fairly strong needle – size 90/14 will do for stitching curtains and is also strong enough for fusible buckram.

Having machine stitched the widths together, take them to the ironing board. Then with the right sides of the curtain fabric together and the seams still unopened, press on the wrong side along the stitches to embed them. After this, lay the material right side down and press the seams open and flat. You will now have a perfect pattern join.

Joining lining widths

The lining widths do not need to be pattern-joined, so they should be simply pinned right sides together and machine stitched 1.5cm (½in) from the edge, using a matching thread. After machine stitching, press the seams to embed the stitches. Then press the seams open and flat in the same way as the curtain material seams.

Hemming lining

Each curtain lining must next be hemmed along the bottom edge. Using the short clear plastic ruler to check the measurement as you proceed, fold 3cm (1¼in) of fabric to the wrong side and press along the fold. Then fold the 3cm (1¼in) over again to double the hem, and press again along the new fold. With the wrong side of the lining facing up, machine stitch close to the top edge of the hem and then press to embed the stitches.

Joining interlining widths

The interlining widths for each curtain are joined in a different way from the lining and curtain materials. Overlap the widths 1.5cm (½in), one on top of the other, and machine stitch them together, using a large zigzag stitch, down the middle of the overlapped fabric. This method minimizes the bulk. Do not hem the interlining in the way you did the lining.

INTERLINING THE CURTAIN

The interlining is used to give definite body and depth to the folds of the curtain material, and for this reason it must be securely, but invisibly, linked to the curtain material. This is done with interlocking stitches, which are worked by hand.

Interlocking the two layers

1 Clamp the interlining onto the table with the top along one end of the table and with one selvedge running lengthwise along the very edge of the table.

2 Gently smooth out the interlining. Then manoeuvre the curtain material (clamping it in place as you position it), right side up, on top of

the interlining with its selvedge exactly on top of the interlining selvedge, and the top of the curtain material 8cm (3in) above the interlining, to allow for the turn-down for the pencil-pleat heading. This will mean that the bottom edges of the two pieces will be approximately lined up, the curtain material having been cut 8cm (3in) longer. Do not worry if the bottom edges vary a little.

3 With the interlining and the material clamped firmly together, fold the material back on itself 40cm (15¾in) from the clamped selvedge. Ensure that the fold runs straight and parallel to the table edge. The curtain material is now in position (see below) to begin the first line of interlocking stitches 40cm (15¾in) from the selvedge.

4 Thread a long darner needle with a strong thread that matches the curtain fabric. Begin the interlocking stitches 20cm (8in) below the top of the interlining and end the stitching 20cm (8in) from the bottom of curtain, so that it will not get in the way of the turnings for headings and hems. First secure the thread to the interlining and a few strands of curtain material at the fold. Then, about 13cm (5in) farther along the fold, insert the needle from front to back through the interlining and then to the front again through the interlining and the curtain material. Pick up only a few strands of the curtain material with each stitch (see below).

5 To complete the interlocking stitch, pass the needle from bottom to top under the strand between this stitch and the previous stitch, then over the working thread. Pull the thread through to complete the 'interlock', but leaving a loose loop of thread between stitches and not pulling stitches tight (see diagram on page 46). Continue in this way, working an interlocking stitch every 13cm (5in) and leaving loose loops between stitches. The stitches will eventually be hidden in folds of the curtain, so do not worry about their being visible. Unclamp the curtain when you have worked down the length of the table, move it along the table, re-clamp and continue stitching to within 20cm (8in) of the end of the curtain.

6 After working the first line of interlocking stitches, starting at the top of the curtain again, smooth

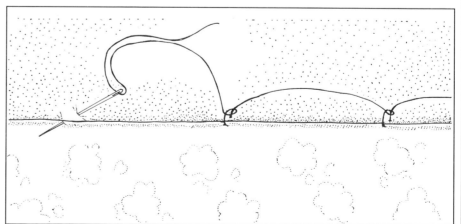

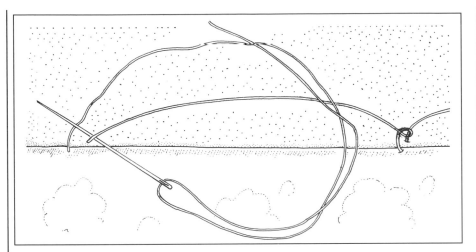

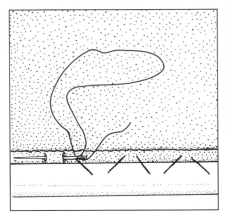

interlining along the edge of the curtain material, again beginning 30cm (11¾in) from the top. Do not let your stitches go through to the front of the curtain. You will find that working these large stitches is very easy if the curtain is clamped to your right and left as you stitch.

Readjust the clamps as necessary, pulling more of the curtain onto the table after you have worked along the whole length of the table. Continue in this way, sewing the curtain material to the interlining and ending the stitches 30cm (11¾ in) from the bottom of the curtain.

5 After finishing the turn-back on the first side edge of the curtain, unclamp the curtain and pull it with its interlining over the table. As you pull the curtain over, continue to firmly stroke the interlining into place with the palms of your hands, checking that its upper edge remains evenly 8cm (3in) below that of the curtain material (do not worry if this varies a little). Align the other side edge of the curtain with the table edge, then turn back and handstitch as for the first side edge of curtain in steps 1–4.

Curtain hem
The curtain is now ready for hemming. This should never be left until last. You may be tempted to hang your curtains and then hem them, but this is totally wrong. The hemming is part of the process of firmly fixing the interlining to the curtain material. So long as you have very carefully calculated your curtain drop, your curtains will be exactly the right length once they are finished.

more curtain material over the interlining and fold back again 40cm (16in) from the last line of interlocking. Then work the second line of interlocking stitches in the same way. Continue in this way working a line of interlocking stitches down the curtain about every 40cm (16in) across the width of the curtain, unclamping and pulling more interlining onto the table as required and working the last line of interlocking stitches about 40cm (16in) from the other edge of the curtain.

7 Once the interlocking has been completed it is advisable to put a few pins through the curtain material and interlining along the top and down the seam joins. This ensures that the interlining will stay in place while the curtain is manoeuvred. Eventually, once the lining has been interlocked in place, the layers will be secure.

Turn-backs at sides of curtain
After the interlining has been interlocked to the curtain material, the side edges of the curtain can be turned to the wrong side and stitched in place. The interlining and the curtain material are each turned back and stitched separately. Now that the curtain material is interlined you will have to move the curtain gently and with great 'respect'.

Turning back side edges of curtain
1 Turn the interlined curtain right side down on the table, with the interlining facing up and with the top of the curtain at one end of the table and one side edge of the curtain running along the length of the table edge. Fold 5cm (2in) of the interlining to the wrong side all along the side edge, so that 5cm (2in) of the curtain material extends out past the fold of the interlining. Pin the interlining as you go.

2 Thread a long darner with thread matching the curtain material and, beginning 30cm (11¾in) from the top of the curtain material, stitch along the very edge of the pinned and folded interlining. Each stitch must go through to the right side of the material but pick up only a few strands of material each time. Space the small running stitches about 4cm–5cm (1½in–2in) apart. Do not pull the stitches too tight or they will 'pit' the curtain material and pucker the edge of the curtain. Stitch in this way down the whole length of the curtain, ending about 30cm (11¾in) from the bottom of the curtain and removing the pins as you go. If the stitches went all the way to the top and bottom of the curtain, you would have to cut them away when you come to turning up the hems and turning down the tops.

3 Now go back to the top of the curtain again, and fold the 5cm (2in) of the curtain material which extends past the interlining over the folded, stitched interlining. Gently pull the curtain to the table edge and clamp it along the length of the table, so that you will not need to pin.

4 Using large diagonal stitches, sew the curtain material to the

Your curtains will hang better if you use lead weights in the hem. You will need only a few weights – one in each corner and one at the base of any seam joining curtain material widths. The type of lead weight that I recommend is a 3cm (1⅛in) flat round weight. Other types of weights will not be nearly so satisfactory.

Hemming the curtain

1 Again manoeuvring the curtain with great respect, move the whole curtain so that the hem end runs along the length of the table, keeping the curtain face down. Moving is facilitated by folding the curtain before trying to turn it. Once it is in place it can be unfolded and then left to drop off the far edge of the table. Smooth the fabric out gently and turn up 12cm (4¾in) along the bottom edge of the curtain for the hem, folding the curtain material and the interlining together. Pin horizontally along the edge at the fold, measuring as you go. The interlining may not be completely even at this stage, but this is irrelevant since it is trimmed back a bit in the next step.

2 Once the entire length of the hem has been pinned, pull back the curtain material only, leaving the

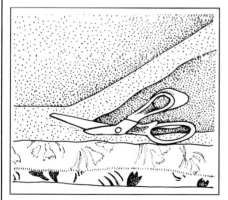

interlining flat. Evenly trim about 4cm (1½in) off the edge of the interlining, so that it measures about 8cm (3in) from the fold in the hem.

3 Once the interlining has been trimmed, smooth the curtain material back over the interlining and turn about 4cm (1½in) *under* the edge of the interlining. Pin this folded edge in place, ending about

25cm (10in) from each side of the curtain to prevent them from being in the way when you are making the corners. Remove the pins along the lower edge of the hem close to the corners, but do not sew the hem yet.

4 You are now ready to make the corners of the hem. Move one corner so that it is lined up with the corner of the table. Check that the folded-up hem and the stitched side edge of the curtain meet to form a perfect right angle by aligning it with the corner of the table. If necessary, adjust the corner to make it a perfect right angle. After this, slip a closed pair of scissors into the middle of the hem fold (between the two layers of interlining) and pull firmly to smooth out any rucks in the fabrics. Next, at the exact point of the corner, stick a pin

through the curtain material and the interlining.

5 Then open out the curtain hem and side turn-back until they lie flat on the table with the interlining opened out, carefully keeping the pin in place. You must next trim away the unwanted excess *interlining*. The sharper your scissors are, the more smoothly this operation will go. When trimming, first clip up from the lower edge to the pin, about 5cm (2in) from the edge of the interlining, ending just a *fraction* beyond the pin. Then clip the interlining from the side edge to the pin to release the 5cm (2in) strip you have just clipped. Lastly cut away the interlining diagonally across the corner forming a perfect right angle to the fold of the hem,

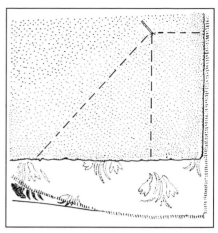

then cut across the interlining that extends past the fold at the hem. (The dotted lines in the illustration above indicate the cutting lines just described.)

6 Now the corner can be folded in position. First fold 5cm (2in) of the side edge of the curtain to the wrong side all along the edge, from where the stitching stopped to the very bottom of the curtain. Then, keeping the side edge folded, fold the curtain material over the diagonal edge of the interlining to

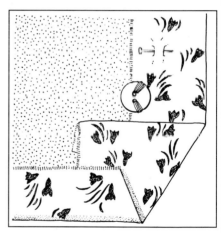

form a perfect right angle. The diagram shows the position of the lead wieght within the corner, but do not sew it in yet.

7 Fold the hem up again, turning the raw edge under the interlining at the top of the hem. Pin along the diagonal of the corner, but do not pin it to the curtain directly below the diagonal. This is because you must now sew the 3cm (1⅛in) lead weight in place so that it will not be visible once the corner is folded up.

When stitching the lead weight to the corner, be careful not to stitch through to the front of the curtain, but only through the interlining. Also, do not place the lead weight at the very fold of the bottom of the hem, but just above it. Once the lead weight is in place, fold the corner back over it and pin the corner securely in place.

8 Make the second corner in the same way, again sewing a lead weight under the edge of the diagonal at the corner before pinning the corner of the hem securely in place. Then sew a lead weight to the base of any seam in the curtain material where two widths have been joined, unpinning the hem temporarily and placing the weight between the two layers of interlining and just above the fold of the hem. Remove all of the pins along the bottom fold of the hem.

9 Sewing from right to left, slipstitch the hem in place, beginning by stitching up the diagonal at the first corner, then working across the entire hem and ending at the end of the diagonal of the second corner.

The stitches must *not* go through to the front of the curtain. Check that the side edges of the curtain are stitched in place all the way to the hem, and complete if necessary. Remove all pins along the hem.

LINING THE CURTAIN
After the side edges and the hem of the curtain have been stitched in place the lining can be sewn on. It is first stitched to the curtain along one side edge, then interlocked to the curtain and finally stitched to the

other side edge of the curtain.

There is no need to stitch the lining to the curtain all the way along its hem, because the lining will be stitched to the curtain hem with every line of interlocking stitches. This is perfectly adequate, especially if you dress the curtains correctly (see page 52).

Sewing lining to curtain
1 Keeping the curtain wrong side facing upwards on the table, manoeuvre the curtain gently in place so that one side edge is running right along the very edge of the length of the table and the lower edge is running along one end of the table. Clamp the curtain to the table in this position. Place the lining right side up on top of the curtain so that the finished hem of the lining (see page 45) is about 3cm (1¼in) from the lower edge of the curtain and so that the side edge of the lining is aligned exactly with the finished side edge of the curtain. Then fold under about 3cm (1¼in) of lining along the side edge of curtain, so that it leaves about 3cm (1¼in) of curtain material exposed between the lining fold and the fold at the side edge of the curtain. The corner of the lining should meet the diagonal fold of the curtain corner. Pin the lining in position as you fold the raw edge under, all along the side edge of the curtain.

2 Slipstitch the lining to the curtain along the pinned side edge, stitching only to within 30cm (11¾in) of the raw edge of the curtain material at the top of the curtain. At the hem of the lining,

stitch only about 2cm (¾in) of the lining to the curtain along the lower edge of the lining. Remove the pins as you stitch.

3 You must now interlock the lining to the curtain. Smooth the lining out over the interlining from the edge of the lining just stitched. Measure about 40cm (15¾in) from this edge of the lining and lay the unfolded 2m (6ft) ruler here, parallel to the

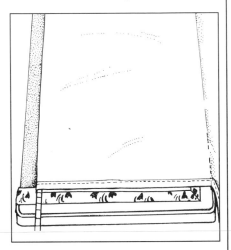

curtain edge. Keeping the ruler in this position, fold the lining back over the ruler. Remove the ruler, without disturbing the fold.

4 Interlock the lining to the curtain all along the fold in the same way that the curtain material was interlocked to the interlining (see steps 4 and 5 on page 45), but working the interlocking stitches about 12cm (4¾in) apart. With each stitch you should prick the needle down through the interlining and back up so that the stitch goes firmly through the interlining, but be careful not to go through the front of the curtain material. Work the stitches to within 20cm (8in) of the edge of the interlining at the top of the curtain; and at the hem of the lining firmly sew the lining to the curtain hem with a few stitches.

5 Work more lines of interlocking stitches across the width of the lining about 40cm (15¾in) apart in the same way.

6 Once the interlocking is complete, trim the side edge of the lining so that it is even with the edge of the finished curtain. Turn under 3cm (1¼in) of the lining as for the first side edge, and slipstitch it in place.

THE CURTAIN HEADING

The curtain heading is the last part of the curtain to be worked. This part of the curtain will vary according to the type of heading you are making. For the pencil-pleat heading the raw edge of the top of the curtain fabric is folded to the wrong side and the pencil-pleat tape is machine stitched in place over it.

The pencil-pleat tape used for the sample curtains is 8cm (3¼in) wide and has three cords which are pulled to form the narrow 'pleats'.

Making the pencil-pleat heading
1 With the curtain still wrong side up on the table and one side edge of the curtain along the length of the table, measure up along the beginning of the lining, from the bottom of the curtain to what you have calculated as the *exact finished curtain drop* of your curtains. Then make a pencil mark for the top of the curtain on the lining. Do this at the other side edge of the curtain and at intervals across the width, in order to achieve a straight edge at the top of the curtain. Then turn the curtain so that the top runs the length of the table. Using the folding ruler and a pencil, draw a line along the lining joining the marks.

2 Taking care not to cut the curtain material, cut the lining and the interlining along the line that you have drawn along the top of the lining. The lining and the interlining now end just at the top (finished) edge of the curtain, and the curtain material will be folded to the wrong side right along this edge.

3 At this stage complete the stitching along the side edges to the top of the trimmed lining. Then trim the curtain material to within 7cm (2¾in) (sufficient for a pencil-pleat heading only) of the newly trimmed edges of the lining and interlining.

4 Fold the excess 7cm (2¾in) of curtain material to the wrong side of the curtain over the lining, folding the corners in diagonally (see

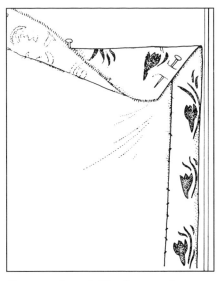

diagram above). Pin the curtain material in place so that the pins are inserted vertically with their heads sticking up beyond the top of the curtain. This is so that they can be removed after the heading tape has been machine stitched to the curtain.

5 There is no need to pin the pencil-pleat tape to the top of the curtain, as you will find it very easy to machine stitch it on without pins. Move your curtain to the machine, taking care not to crease it. At the beginning of the tape pull out the 3 cords to enable you to turn under about 1.5cm (½in) of the beginning

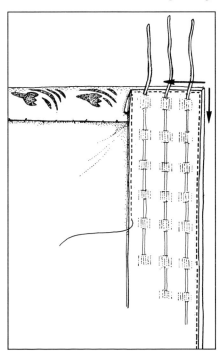

of the tape. Place the *wrong side* of the tape (the hook pockets are on the right side) on the wrong side of the curtain so that it covers the raw edge of the curtain fabric. The folded-under end of the tape should begin as close as possible to the side edge of the curtain without showing at the front. The long edge of the pencil-pleat tape should also be as close as possible to the top edge of the curtain without showing. (In effect, the tape should be about 1mm or 2mm from the edge of the curtain.) Using a matching thread, first machine stitch all along the top edge of the tape, close to the edge of the tape, through all thicknesses. When you reach within 7cm (3in) of the end of the curtain, pull out the 3 cords, trim the tape and fold the end under as at the beginning. Then complete the stitching along this first edge of the tape, turn a right angle and stitch down the folded-under end of the tape. Go back to the beginning of the tape and machine stitch across the folded end of the tape, then turn a right angle and stitch along the side of the tape, again stitching close to the edge of the tape. The pencil-pleat tape is now machine-stitched to the curtain along all four of its sides. You can now remove the pins along the top of the curtain.

6 The next step is to gather up the heading. This can be quite strenuous work, but here again your wonderful clamps can help. Clamp one end of the heading to the table; this will give you something to pull against. Take hold of the 3 cords in the tape and pull up the curtain to the desired width to cover half the window, the housing space, the return at the outside edge of the curtain and the overlap at the leading edge (see *Finished width of pleated curtain* on page 37). Pull up from both ends evenly until the desired width is achieved. After you have finished gathering, knot the 3 cords securely together at the leading edge. At the outside edge of the curtain, knot the 3 cords only loosely so that you can release them to adjust the width if necessary when the curtains are finally hanging in place.

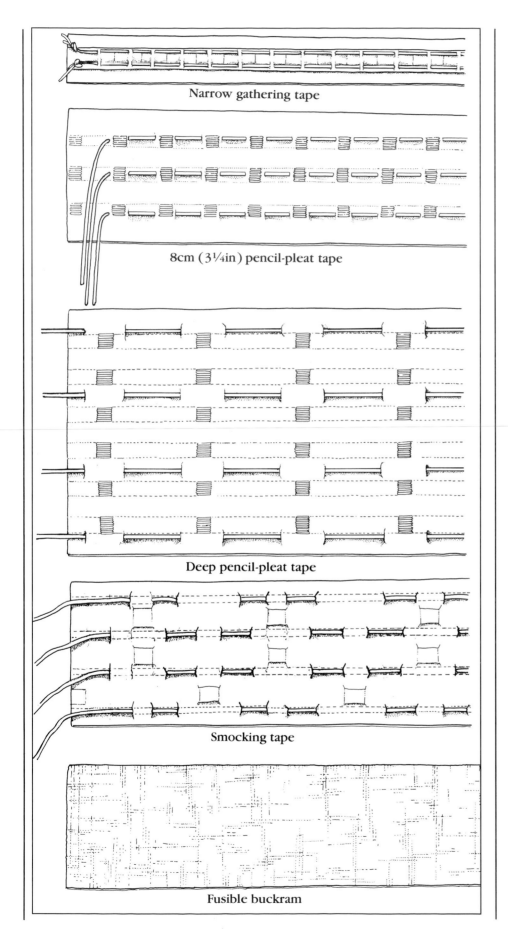

Narrow gathering tape

8cm (3¼in) pencil-pleat tape

Deep pencil-pleat tape

Smocking tape

Fusible buckram

7 Now insert a brass curtain hook in every 4th pocket all along the pulled-up pencil-pleat tape.

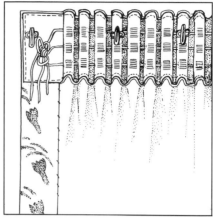

HEADING TAPES AND BUCKRAM

The heading you make for your curtains, pelmet or blind is an important part of your finished window treatment. You should only ever use the very best heading tapes. In order to ensure that my curtains and pelmets have the most professional headings possible, I only use the best-quality pencil-pleat tape. For French- or goblet-pleat headings I insert fusible buckram in the heading and make the pleats by hand. This ensures truly crisp pleats that will hold their body indefinitely. The curtains or pelmet will hang beautifully from this type of stiffened pleat.

If you want a professional finish, avoid tapes that promise to form large pleats for you. They will never have the crispness and clarity of handmade pleats made with fusible buckram, especially if used on an elegantly deep interlined curtain or pelmet.

Narrow gathering tape
Narrow gathering tape is usually about 2cm (¾in) wide and it is the tape I use when making a ruched pair of swags (see *Ruched swags and tails* on page 92).

Because it is not strong enough to bear the weight of heavy interlined curtains, I never use it for curtains. The only time I would use it, other than for ruched swags, is for little gathered skirts on dressing tables or for coronas above beds.

8cm (3¼in) pencil-pleat tape
For most of the curtains I design, which are to go behind a pelmet, I use an 8cm (3¼in)-wide pencil-pleat tape for the heading. Although this tape is·not designed for an exposed curtain heading which is going to be drawn every day, it is fine for curtains covered by a pelmet. There is no need to make French pleats at the top of a curtain that is covered, because your

It is the fusible buckram interfacing that gives the French pleats on these fixed-headed curtains (below) their tailored, regimented, grand and organized appearance.

Goblet-pleat headings (like the one seen right) must also be interfaced with fusible buckram if crisp, firm pleats are required.

curtains will hang just as well with a pencil-pleat heading, so long as they have been properly dressed (see page 53).

The best type of 8cm (3¼in) pencil-pleat tape is the one with 3 hook pockets, one above the other. You can move the hooks up or down if any alteration is needed in the length of the curtains. This tape also has the advantage of having each pocket subdivided so that there is even more room for manoeuvring the hooks to different levels within each pocket. The pockets are placed 2.5cm (1in) apart all along the tape, and when the three cords running along the tape are pulled up the pockets come forward along the right side of the tape and the spaces between the pockets are pushed backwards towards the front of the curtain.

This width of pencil-pleat tape is also perfect for static headings in a pencil-pleated pelmet (see page 73) or an Austrian blind (see page 102).

Deep pencil-pleat tape
There is also a deep pencil-pleat tape, 14.5cm (5¾in) wide, which I tend to use on deep pelmets, because the 8cm (3¼in) pencil-pleat tape does not look good on a pelmet that is over 35cm (13¾in) in length. You will find that the deeper pelmet is much better balanced by using a deep pencil-pleat tape.

This wider tape has a vertical row of 6 pockets at equal intervals along it. The rows of pockets are spaced slightly farther apart than 3-pocket rows on the 8cm (3¼in)-wide tape.

Smocking tape
Smocking tape is designed for pelmets only. It has a stunning effect especially when, after being pulled up, it is simply hand-smocked with 6 strands of stranded embroidery floss (see page 75). Again, when buying smocking tape, make an effort to find the best quality available. Inferior smocking tapes will not form the diamond shapes properly when pulled up.

Fusible buckram
Fusible buckram is a stiff, firm interfacing fabric used to stiffen the headings of curtains and pelmets

made with French and goblet pleats (see *Glossary* on page 130 for an alternative for fusible buckram). It is also used for those pelmets with a piped band about 12cm (5in) wide with gathered or pleated 'skirts' coming off them.

Buckram comes in rolls and is usually available in Britain in three widths – 10cm (4in), 12.5cm (5in) and 15cm (6in). It is wonderful stuff because it tears easily in a straight line, so if you have only a roll of the widest width you can tear it to a narrower width with ease as you unroll it.

When the buckram is used in a heading it is placed between the interlining and the lining and then pressed. The pressing permanently glues it in position. Never make the mistake of placing a hot iron directly onto the buckram because of its

The fixed heading on this window treatment (above) enhances the beauty of the deep smocking. Note how the pretty coral colour of the material contrasts with the white view.

heavy glue content. It must always be ironed with the lining covering it completely on the top and with the interlining under it. In this way the glue touches neither the curtain fabric nor the iron.

HANGING AND DRESSING CURTAINS
Once you have finished your curtains you should try to hang them as soon as possible to prevent creasing. However, if there is a delay they can survive perfectly well for weeks, lying on a very clean floor or hanging over a banister, preferably covered with a dust sheet. After the

curtains are hanging you will need to 'dress' them.

'Dressing' is the final touch which will give your curtains their highly professional look. Until being made into curtains, curtain material, interlining and lining have only ever been either rolled up on bolts or laid out on tables. After having carefully sewn all three component parts together, it is essential that you now arrange the curtains into regular pleats. Properly dressed, the lining, interlining and curtain material will behave as one body forever after, going backwards and forwards across the window in one fluid movement.

One thing to remember, however, is that curtains, once dressed, can be upset by a window that is frequently left wide open. The draught causes the curtains to billow out, which is very bad for them. This is why curtains should be able to be drawn well clear of an open window to avoid upsetting the perfect pleats. I would recommend the use of tie backs to control dressed curtains in front of a frequently opened window or door.

Hanging the curtains
1 Never hang curtains when alone in the house, and preferably not even alone in the room. Accidents can happen. Begin by counting the number of hooks on the curtain to see if they correspond to the number of runners on the rod, including the overlap arm and the screw eyes at the corners of the pelmet board (see page 40). To adjust the number of runners, open the gate at either end of the curtain rod and feed on or remove runners until the number is correct. (This process is clearly described in the manufacturer's instructions.)

2 Climb the ladder with one curtain over your shoulder and begin hooking the curtain to the runners at one end of the pelmet board. Do not begin in the centre of the rod, because the whole weight of the curtain should never hang solely from the overlap arm.

3 Hang the second curtain in the same way as the first.

4 Once both curtains have been hung, check that they overlap at the middle and hug the wall at the ends. If necessary, readjust the pleats by pulling them up or releasing some of the cord until the closed curtains are perfectly gathered. Then at each outside edge of each curtain, knot the 3 loosely tied cords together securely. Make sure that no cords are hanging down and showing at the front of the curtain. You can roll these long ends up and sew the roll to the inside of the curtain.

Dressing the curtains
1 Having hung the curtains, cut 10 pieces of string, or strips of left-over fabric, each long enough to tie around the curtain when the curtains are drawn open.

2 Open the curtains fully. Then begin pleating the curtains with your hands at about chest level. Stand sideways to the window and close to the right-hand curtain looking towards its outside edge. Place your left hand behind the leading edge of the curtain, so that it points towards the window. (The leading edge *must* point towards the window.) Keeping your hands stretched out and flat so that the fingertips will push out each fold of the pleat, place your right hand behind your left hand, on the right side of the curtain, thus forming the second pleat fold – towards the window. As you form a pleat, first

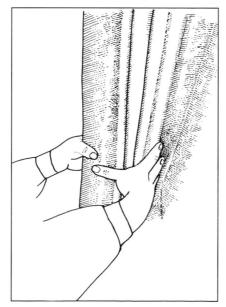

with one hand and then with the other, press the pleated section of the curtain onto your chest to keep the pleats stacked up on top of each other. The depth of the pleats depends on the size of the window. The bigger the window, the deeper the pleats should be. Pleat across the whole curtain in this way. If you end up with the outside edge of the curtain turning towards the room with the lining showing, simply re-pleat the curtains, making the pleats slightly deeper or shallower.

3 Once you have pleated all the way across the curtain, tie a piece of string or a strip of fabric around it. Tie it so that it is tight enough to really hold the pleats firmly but not so tight that it creases the material.

4 Now climb the ladder and repeat the pleating process at the very top

Tying the curtain

of the curtain, matching the pleats to those already made below. Pleat again in 3 other positions: halfway between the top and the middle, 10cm (4in) from the bottom of the curtain, and lastly between the hem and the middle. Make sure each time to follow *exactly* the size and position of the first pleats you made in step 2. Dress the other curtain in the same way (see page 53).

5 Having tied up the curtains, I always clap them hard between my hands so that they really get the message! They are very pliable and always respond beautifully. If you can resist closing the curtains, try to leave them tied for at least 4 days. Then, if treated with respect, they will always hang perfectly in their pleats.

ALTERING LENGTH OF CURTAINS ON SITE

If small problems arise with the length of your curtains once they are already hanging, there are many ways of altering the length without having to touch a stitch.

The reason for the incorrect length of your curtains will not, I am sure, be your measuring ability! It could, rather, be one of the following:

– The builders used a different architrave than planned
– The curtains have come from another house or room
– Your pelmet board cannot be fixed in the planned position because of bad plaster
– You have changed your mind about having so much length in your extra-long curtains (see page 32)

All of these problems are easily solvable and none of the alterations that follow will ever be apparent to the onlooker because they are hidden way up behind the pelmet.

Lengthening by moving hooks
If the hook pockets on your heading tape have subdivisions, one way of lengthening your curtains is to move the hook up to the halfway position in the pocket. This will allow your curtains to gain a little length.

Lengthening with spacers
To gain more length you can put 'spacers' between the curtain rod and the pelmet board. A 'spacer' is a wooden disc about 2cm (¾in) in diameter and 8mm (¼in) thick. It has a hole through the centre, so that a screw can be screwed through it. To lower the curtains, place a

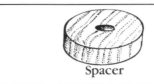
Spacer

spacer between the top-fixing curtain rod and the pelmet board at each screw along the rod. This will, of course, drop the curtain rod only 8mm (¼in), but up to 3 spacers can be stacked on top of each other between the curtain rod and the board.

If you cannot find these spacers (see the list of suppliers on page 128), it is easy enough to make your own from a piece of hardwood dowelling.

Lengthening with S-hooks
The way to gain even more length for your curtains is to use S-hooks. In this method you will need to take the curtains down (but not the curtain rod, as with the spacers).

S-hooks come in 6 sizes – 2cm (¾in), 2.5cm (1in), 2.8cm (1⅛in), 3cm (1¼in), 4cm (1½in) and 5cm (2in). First choose the size that will lengthen your curtains to the desired measurement and buy one S-hook for each curtain hook. Then open one end of each S-hook with a pair of pliers so you can slip it onto a runner where the hooks would normally go. Once the S-hook is in place, close the end again with the

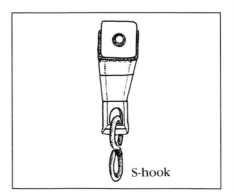
S-hook

pliers or it will be likely to jump off the runner.

After the S-hooks are all in place, insert the curtain hooks into them. A good quality curtain rod will happily accommodate the addition of the S-hooks.

Shortening by moving hooks
If your curtains are too long, the first option you have available is to move the hooks in the tape to a lower pocket. This will raise the curtains considerably. The pencil-

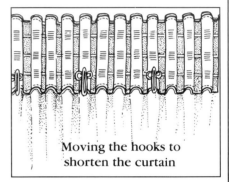
Moving the hooks to shorten the curtain

pleat heading will naturally jut forwards, but this does not matter. The fact that the rod is set in the middle of the pelmet board means that the heading can be easily accommodated without ever disturbing the pelmet.

Raising the pelmet board
The spacers used to drop a curtain rod (see above left) can also be used to raise it. In this instance, however, the spacers are placed between the horizontal arm of the bracket holding the pelmet board to the wall and the pelmet board itself. This raises the board and, with it, the curtain rod, thereby raising the curtains.

The pelmet board can also be raised by attaching it to the wall with slotted adjustable brackets. The pelmet board can then be raised and lowered as desired.

Chapter Five

CURTAIN PROJECTS

If you want a window treatment that does not have a pelmet, you should choose a
curtain heading that will do justice to your overall design. In this chapter I cover
four types of heading that will give elegance to any window treatment without a
pelmet – a French-pleated heading, a goblet-pleated heading (see above), a slotted
heading and a Velcro heading with a stand-up. The best alternatives to a pelmet
board are also explained; these include poles and rings, covered-fascia boards
and brass swing arms.

FRENCH-PLEATED CURTAINS

French pleats (also called pinch pleats) are suitable for the headings of curtains hanging from poles (see page 61) or hanging from a curtain rod hidden by a covered fascia (see page 66).

It is, to me, a total waste of time and effort to French-pleat a curtain whose heading will be hidden under a pelmet. It is a fallacy that curtains hang better when made with French pleats. They do not; if dressed the way I suggest (page 52), they will hang beautifully, regardless of their heading.

The sample curtains

Once again in order to make the instructions as clear as possible for you, I will use the sample curtains as the example. The measurements for the sample window are set out in **Table 2** (see page 36). This time, however, instead of having a pencil-pleat heading, the curtains are to be made with a French-pleated heading.

Cutting length

The finished *flat* width of a French-pleated curtain would be the same as for a pencil-pleated curtain – i.e.

French pleats look good hanging from pole rings (above). This treatment takes advantage of the lovely contrast of the yellow material against the green grass and trees.

1.94m (6ft 4in) for the sample curtains (see *Unsewn single curtain* page 43). But the *cutting length* will be slightly longer.

The turn-down allowance at the top of a French-pleated curtain depends on the length of the pleat. For floor-length curtains I like to use a rather long pleat for elegance and would normally use 15cm (6in) fusible buckram so that I can work 15cm (6in)-long pleats.

The turn-down allowance required for 15cm (6in) buckram is 18cm (7in), which is 8cm (3in) more than the turn-down on a pencil-pleat heading.

By following **Table 4** (page 37), you will see how to determine the cutting length for your French-pleated curtains. Add the curtain drop (see page 62 for measuring the drop from the pole and page 67 for measuring the drop from a board with a covered fascia), the hem and the turn-down at the top. For the sample curtains the result is 3.10m (10ft 2¼in) for the cutting length.

As for the pencil-pleat curtains you will need 1½ widths of material in each curtain, so you will need a total of 3 widths. Always remember to add extra onto the cutting length for the pattern-matching when deciding how much material to purchase. Be generous when you calculate your pattern repeat, or you may end up not having quite enough material.

Cutting and joining the widths
For cutting the curtain material follow the instructions given in Chapter 4 for the pencil-pleated curtains (pages 42–43 steps 1–6).

The instructions for cutting the lining and interlining are the same as for the pencil-pleated curtains (page 43), except that they should be cut 14cm (5½in) shorter than the curtain-material widths.

Join the curtain widths, the lining widths and the interlining widths as described in Chapter 4 (pages 44–45). Note that the lining must be hemmed after the widths are joined.

Making the curtains
1 Begin making the curtains by interlocking the curtain material to the interlining. Follow steps 1–7 on page 46 for interlocking, but in step 2 position the top of the curtain material 14cm (5½in) *above* the interlining.

2 Then turn back and hand stitch the side edges of the curtain, following steps 1–5 on page 46, but with the important difference of beginning the stitches 36cm (14in) below the top of the curtain instead of 30cm (11¾in) in steps 2 and 5, so as to leave room for inserting the fusible buckram.

3 After turning back the edges, hem the curtains, following steps 1–9 on pages 47 and 48.

4 Sew the lining to the curtain, following steps 1–6 (page 48), but in step 2 work the stitches to within 36cm (14in) of the raw edge of the curtain material at the top.

The curtain heading
The biggest difference between making pencil-pleated curtains and French-pleated curtain is, of course, the heading itself.

For the French-pleated heading you must iron on the fusible buckram before turning down the excess curtain material over the lining. The iron should be fairly hot, and you will need to press the buckram on your work table rather than on the ironing board. So put an extension cord on your iron, and pad your table if necessary, before beginning step 2 below.

You may not need to pad the table, as a layer of curtain material and a layer of interlining will be between the table and the iron. But depending on how valuable your table is, you may need to protect it further before ironing on it.

Making the French-pleat heading
1 Measure the finished drop, measuring up from the bottom edge of the curtain as for the pencil-pleat curtains, step 1 and 2 (page 49).

2 Now fold back 5cm (2in) of the side edges of the interlining and curtain material which were unstitched and pin in place. Leave the lining free. This is so that the buckram can be slipped in between the interlining and the interlining turn-back.

3 Now unroll some of the fusible buckram, and slip it between the lining and the interlining, either side up. Cut off the amount of buckram you need. The edge of the buckram should be lined up with

the top of the curtain – i.e. the raw edges of the interlining and the lining – and tucked under the side seam turn-backs at each end, so that it goes up to the very edges. With the lining smoothed out over the buckram, clamp the curtain heading to the table so that the edges of the buckram, lining and interlining run along the long edge of the table. Finish the stitching of lining to the curtain material along the side edges to the top of the lining.

4 Press the buckram in place, first making sure that it is completely covered by the interlining on one

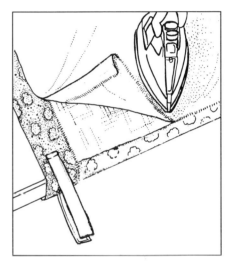

side and by the lining on the other. You do not want either the curtain material or the iron to come in contact with the glue in the fusible buckram.

5 Having inserted the buckram along the full width of the curtain, you can now fold the excess curtain material at the top to the wrong side over the lining. There should be about 18cm (7in) of curtain material extending beyond the top of the lining, but do not worry if this varies a little. Pull the curtain material tightly so as to achieve a very sharp edge. Press along the fold.

6 Now turn under about 3cm (1in) along the raw edge of the curtain material so that the fold is about level with the bottom edge of the buckram. Pin this folded-under edge in place, and then at the corners fold back a diagonal corner as for the heading of the pencil-pleat

curtains (see diagram in step 4 on page 49). Pin this fold in place and press, *but do not stitch* it. Stitching is unnecessary, as the pleats made along the heading will hold the hem in place. Only the corners are slipstitched in place after pleating.

Calculating pleated curtain width
You *must* allow a little extra in the final pleated width measurement of each curtain when using fusible buckram in a heading. The buckram has no 'give' whatsoever, and there is no way of altering the finished width of the curtain heading once the pleats have been made. This means that there is no room for error, unlike the case with pencil-pleat tape, which is very forgiving because of its gathering cords.

The reason you need a little extra in fusible-buckram-headed curtains is that the buckram must be allowed to bulge outwards or inwards (very slightly) between the pleats. It should not be stretched tight and flat. I usually add 15cm (6in) for the extra allowance for each curtain, whether it is made up of one or three widths. This applies to a French-pleated heading hanging from a pole and from a curtain rod on a board with a covered fascia.

For the sample curtain you will see in **Table 3** (page 36) that the finished width of the curtain after pleating is 82.5cm (2ft 8½in). Adding 15cm (6in) extra onto this

width will bring the required width for the French-pleated sample curtain to 97.5cm (38½in).

The extra added would obviously not apply to a pelmet with French pleats, because that is a static heading which is supposed to be fixed fairly tightly across the board.

Calculating for pleats
The diagram below shows the pleat positions and pleat width for the sample curtain. This is a fairly simple process, but you may find it easier if you draw it to scale on graph paper as you make your calculations.

First determine how much *excess* there is for the pleats by subtracting the finished width from the flat curtain width. For the sample curtains:

$$194\text{cm} - 97.5\text{cm} = 96.5\text{cm}$$
$$(76\text{in} - 38\tfrac{1}{2}\text{in} = 37\tfrac{1}{2}\text{in})$$

You should allow between 10cm (4in) and 15cm (6in) for each pleat, so you will want, in this instance, 8 pleats.

$$96.5\text{cm} \div 8 = 12\text{cm}$$
$$(37\tfrac{1}{2}\text{in} \div 8 = 4\tfrac{3}{4}\text{in})$$

These calculations do, of course, have to be rounded off, and you will have to come as close as possible to your finished curtain width without worrying about being a fraction off.

Next calculate the width of the gap between the pleats. The first and last pleat should be placed about 5cm (2in) from the ends of the curtain. So subtract this from the finished width:

$$97.5\text{cm} - 10\text{cm} = 87.5\text{cm}$$
$$(38\tfrac{1}{2}\text{in} - 4\text{in} = 34\tfrac{1}{2}\text{in})$$

Now divide the amount you have left after subtracting the gaps at the ends by the number of gaps between the pleats. With 8 pleats you will have 7 gaps between pleats, therefore:

$$87.5\text{cm} \div 7 = 12.5\text{cm}$$
$$(34\tfrac{1}{2}\text{in} \div 7 = 5\text{in})$$

The gaps between the pleats will therefore measure 12.5cm (5in).

Clothes pegs and pin hooks
After having calculated the width and positions of your pleats, you are ready to make them. Sprung clothes pegs (U.S. 'clothes-pins') are used to hold the pleats in place before stitching and are an essential tool when making pleats with buckram.

The type of curtain hook needed for French pleats is larger than that used with pencil-pleat headings. It is called a *pin hook* and is not sewn to the heading; instead, the sharp end of the hook is literally 'stabbed' through the material on the wrong side of the heading.

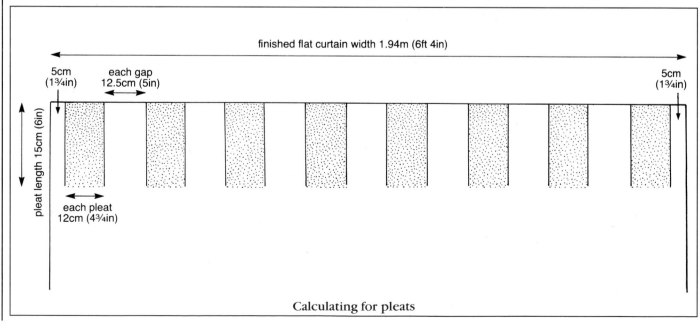

finished flat curtain width 1.94m (6ft 4in)

5cm (1¾in)

each gap 12.5cm (5in)

5cm (1¾in)

pleat length 15cm (6in)

each pleat 12cm (4¾in)

Calculating for pleats

Making the French pleats

1 With the wrong side of the curtain facing up, mark out each pleat with 2 vertically inserted pins, one at each side of the pleat. The pinheads should stick up above the top of the curtain. Move the pins on the wrong side, along the lower edge of the turn-down, to positions in the *gaps* between the pleats. This is essential, otherwise they will either get in the way of the stitching of the pleats or get lost in the pleat once made. The pinheads in the gaps must be pointing *downwards*.

2 Now fold the pleats wrong side together so that the two pinheads marking out the pleat are aligned. Use a sprung clothes peg to hold the pleat in place. I tend to peg one at a time, machine stitch it and then move on to the next.

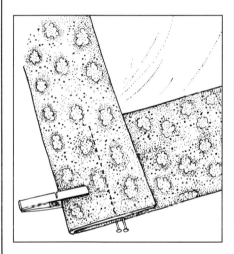

3 Having pegged the pleat, machine stitch down the side of it. Remove the pins marking the pleat just before stitching. Then line up your short ruler along the line of the side of the pleat, and gently scratch the line into the material along the ruler, ending at the bottom of the buckram, 15cm (6in) from the top of the curtain. Start stitching about 1cm (¼in) from the top of the curtain, going backwards over the top of the curtain, then reverse and stitch forwards down the length of the pleat to the bottom of the buckram. At the end of the buckram again go backwards and forwards to secure the stitching. Cut off excess threads at the seam ends very close to the stitches. You will see that the reason for not starting the machine

stitching at the very top of the curtain is so that there will be no unsightly ends sticking up above the curtain. Machine stitch the remaining pleats in the same way.

4 Next lay the curtain wrong side down and flat on the table with its top edge lying towards you. Hold one pleat along the fold in the middle of the pleat with the finger-tips of both hands – one hand should hold the pleat at the very bottom of the machine stitching and the other at the top (there is only one hand in the diagram, so as not to obscure the forming folds). Push the pleat downwards towards the table (and the seam), so that the sides bulge outwards, and the whole pleat now forms into 3 smaller pleats. The centre pleat should stick out only fractionally less than the two equal side pleats. Pinch the 3 pleats together and peg them at the top.

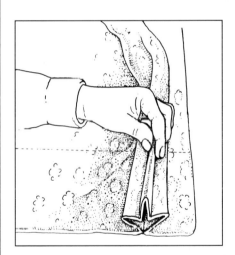

5 Thread a needle with a doubled matching thread. Knot the end of the threads firmly, and insert the needle in between 2 of the 3 pleats *just* below the buckram, so that the knot will be hidden. Pull the needle out on one side of the triple pleats, halfway between the folded edge of the pleat and the machine stitching, again just below the buckram. Now, to secure the base of the pleat, work 3 or 4 stab stitches (vertically worked running stitches) firmly through all the layers of the pleats, working towards the front edge of the pleat. (You have to work the stitches just below the buckram because it is impossible to go

through the buckram.) End the stitches 3mm (⅛in) from the edge of the pleat, as the front edges of the pleat should not be oversewn. The triple folds look much neater with no stitching overlapping them.

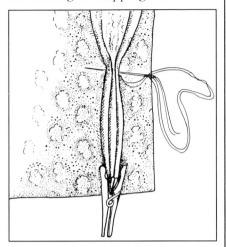

6 Repeat steps 4 and 5, sewing each pleat at the base as for the first. Leave the pegs in the tops of the pleats for 2 to 3 days to make the pleat tops very sharp.

7 On the wrong side, slipstitch the corners of the heading fold in place.

8 Before hanging the curtains, 'stab' one pin hook into the back of the heading at each pleat, running the 'pin' up one side of the pleat seam. Also insert one hook at each end of the curtain. The tops of the hooks should be 1.5cm (½in) below the top of the curtain if the curtain is being hung from a ring on a wooden pole, or 5.5cm (2¼in) below if it is being hung from a board with a covered fascia.

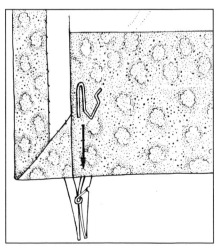

should always be about 3cm (1in) more than the width of the fusible buckram.

Making the goblet pleats

1 First work steps 1, 2 and 3 as for *Making the French pleats* (see page 59).

2 Pinch the first pleat together and into 3 sections as for the French pleat in step 4, but only at the base of the pleat, *not at the top*.

3 Sew the pleat across the base as for the French pleat in step 5.

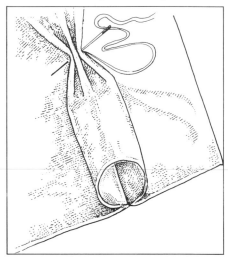

4 Pinch each pleat together and hand sew through it at the base as for the first pleat.

5 On the wrong side, slipstich the corners of the heading fold in place.

6 Stuff each pleat *generously* with scraps of interlining so that it will hold its goblet shape.

7 Insert the pin hooks as for the French pleats in step 8.

Goblet pleats with buttons

You may wish to draw attention to your goblet-pleated heading by adding contrasting details to it. Goblet pleats look superb with a covered button stitched to the base of each pleat. Use a contrast for the buttons so that they stand out at a distance (see facing page).

'Squared-off' goblet pleats

For a different effect the shape of the pleat can be altered slightly to

GOBLET-PLEATED CURTAINS

Goblet pleats (U.S. 'French pleats') give a lovely, bold effect along the top of your curtains. Because the pleats are pinched together into 3 sections only at the base and left open at the top, they look best if they are about 10cm–12cm (4in–4½in) long, unlike the French pleat, which has a better appearance if it is 15cm (6in) long.

The goblet-pleated curtains are made in exactly the same way as the

Because these curtains (above) have a fixed heading, the goblet pleats can be spaced very closely together. An interesting detail on these curtains is the shaped leading edges.

French-pleated curtains, except that the individual pleats are finished off in a slightly different way. Also, if you are making a shorter pleat, remember to match the width of your buckram to the desired length of the pleat. The heading allowance form a 'squared-off' goblet pleat. This is done simply by stitching each side of the top of the pleat to the top edge of the curtain about 1.5cm (½in) from the pleat seam, with one or two overcast stitches. The pleat is then stuffed as for the plain goblet pleat. (The illustration on the right of the swagged cord shows squared-off goblet pleats.)

Goblet pleats with a swagged cord
A cord knotted in a figure-of-8, 'swagging' between each pleat looks so elegant and gives an interesting added dimension (see right).

To do this you should stitch a figure-8 knot to the base of each pleat (see diagram below for making the knot).

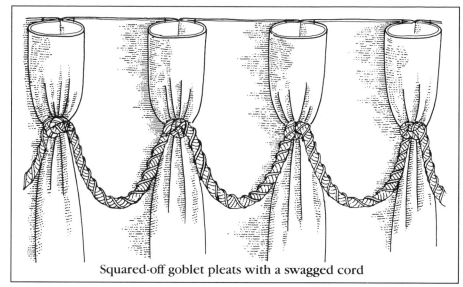

Squared-off goblet pleats with a swagged cord

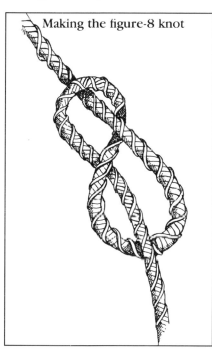

Making the figure-8 knot

Between each pleat let the cord hang down in a graceful loop.

The pleating can be further enhanced by binding both the top and the leading edges of the curtain with a contrasting colour.

POLES WITH RINGS
Poles with rings are a very popular way to hang curtains. I feel that only French and goblet pleats look good hanging from pole rings. These pleats stack up so well, with the buckram heading curving towards the wall between each pleat.

Curtains can also be made with a casing at the top, so that they can be

slotted onto the pole, but this type of curtain cannot be opened and closed like curtains hanging from rings (see page 62).

Types of poles
Pole designs vary enormously, and your final choice of pole will depend on the effect you wish to achieve and the price you are prepared to pay. Because there is such a wide range of poles, take your time in choosing the one you want; you will have to live with it for a long time.

Pole finials
If you are tempted to buy a pole with long finials, remember to check that there is enough width on either side of your window to

accommodate them. Adjacent walls, beams and other architectural features tend to get in the way. I often find this frustrating in the narrow entrance hall found in a classic London house. One longs to curtain-over the glass-panelled door, and a pole would be so suitable. But since the door, and its side panels, fill the entire width of the hall, there is no room for the finials.

Brass poles
Napoleon had a great liking for majestic poles with lovely coloured satins artistically thrown over them. Equally, the Victorians were very proud to display their curtains from regal poles.

The Victorian pole often had extremely decorative finials in the

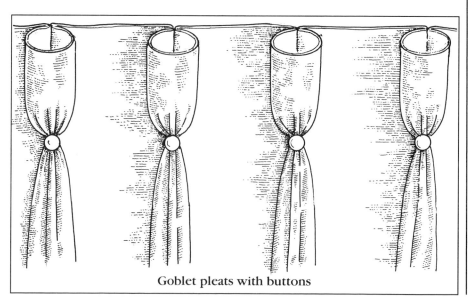

Goblet pleats with buttons

form of pineapples, coronets or ridged balls. These poles would have been made of brass with a 'railway' track pulley system housed in them. You can still buy similar brass poles but they are very expensive; it's better to inherit them!

Plastic 'brass' poles
Because the authentic brass poles are so expensive you can now buy imitation brass poles. They are made of a hard plastic which has a chrome finish in a choice of colours such as 'antique brass', 'bright gold' and 'antique gold'. I have never found these poles to be very sturdy, but they do come with a pulley system and have proper runners – the rings on them being fake.

Wooden poles
There is a huge range of wooden poles available which come in many finishes, including white, natural wood and varnished wood, including mahogany. Wooden poles have solid wooden rings and they come in varying diameters. Their disadvantage is that they do not have a pulley system.

Measuring for the pole length
The length of a pole is determined by adding the housing space (see **Table 1** on page 34) to the width of the window. As mentioned before, be sure that there is room for the finials which will extend past the length of pole needed to accommodate the curtains.

Measuring the drop from a pole
Measuring the finished drop for curtains that are to hang from a pole is not easy when the pole is not already in place. Unlike a pelmet board, which is a flat object, the pole is cylindrical, is fixed with circular brackets and has circular rings, making the measuring process more difficult. Therefore I strongly advise you to fix the pole to the wall and *then* measure the curtain drop.

The easiest way to measure the drop from the pole is to tie a bit of string from the screw eye on the ring. Mark the end of the string right up next to the screw eyes, and cut off the other end of the string where it touches the carpet. Then remove

the string and measure it with the long folding ruler; add 1cm (¼in) so that the curtain will cover the screw eye. This is the finished drop of your curtain. To measure in any other way is difficult, since the rings spin around when you touch them. Also, because the pole is set a distance from the wall (because of its brackets), you have nothing to lean the ruler against.

French or goblet pleats on poles
When hanging French- or goblet-pleated curtains from a pole, be sure that the top of each pin hook is 1.5cm (½in) below the top of the curtain so that the curtain will cover the screw eye.

The outside edge of the curtains must turn a right angle to meet the wall at each end of the pole. This is achieved by screwing a screw eye into the wall at the correct level at each end of the curtain and inserting the last curtain hook on each side into the screw eye. An *extra allowance* for these 'returns' needs to be added to the total finished pleated curtain width.

SLOTTED-HEAD CURTAINS
The slotted-head curtains are made by stitching a channel, or casing, across the top of the curtain several centimetres (one or more inches) below the top edge and slipping the curtain onto a pole. The material gathered onto the pole creates a frilled stand-up above the pole.

Although the curtain heading remains closed, the curtains are drawn back from the window by a tie-back (see page 113). This is a dramatic arrangement for a window treatment and can be so stylish.

I often use this 'fixed head', or 'static', treatment on landing windows, for example, where it is not essential to gain maximum light. Slotted-head curtains can have great impact here because they are not interlined, and the light shining through them really brings out the colour and design of the material. For this reason silk is an excellent choice for such curtains.

Tie-backs and Maltese crosses
Brass roses, or rosettes, or brass hold-backs look good with slotted-

head curtains, but any number of tie-back designs are also effective. I particularly favour ruched tie backs (see page 117) for this window treatment because their design blends beautifully with that of the curtain heading.

A stunning way to finish off the curtains is to place an elegant bow or a Maltese cross (see page 124) in the centre of the heading.

Poles for slotted-head curtains
The length of the pole for these curtains should be the width of the window plus the housing space. The instructions given are for using poles with or without finials. If you are using a pole without finials, the pole itself will then be completely covered and you can use a piece of wooden doweling 3cm (1¼in) in diameter for the pole.

This type of slotted-head curtain also looks marvellous hanging from a brass drop rod 1cm (½in) in diameter.

Curtain length
The curtains should be slightly longer than just to the floor. Because they are basically 'dress' curtains, they are tied back most of the time, which always causes the inner section of both curtains to rise off the floor. This is part of the design and is extremely attractive.

Making the curtains
Slotted-head curtains are made in the same way as the pencil-pleated curtains in Chapter 4 up until making the heading; with the following few exceptions.

First, the interlining should be omitted and the lining should not be interlocked to the curtain material, but stitched all the way to the top of the curtain all along the side edges. Also the two curtains together should be 3 times the length of the pole, so that when the heading is fed onto the pole you will get a tightly ruched look. For this you need plenty of fullness.

These slotted-head curtains with a stand-up (right) have great impact which is enhanced by the stunning silk Roman blind (see page 107 for how to make Roman blinds).

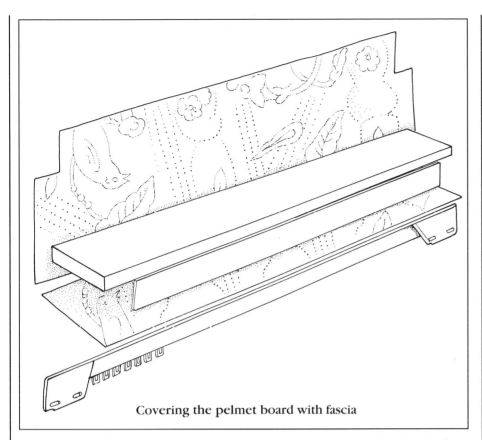

Covering the pelmet board with fascia

drop should be measured from the *top* of the board, not from the bottom. This is because the top of the curtains must be level with the top of the board when hanging.

Making the board with fascia

1 Using a suitable wood glue, glue the 5cm (2in)-wide Formica to the 2cm (¾in) edge of the board so that it begins and ends 7cm (2¾in) from the ends of the board and so that the top edge of the Formica is level with the top edge of the board. The Formica is shorter than the board to accommodate the ends of the curtain rod, which on some types of rod project forward. Check your rod before gluing to make sure that this measurement allows enough space. The rod is going to sit flush with the front of the board. Do not screw the rod on yet.

2 Once the glue has dried, cover the board and the fascia with curtain material, using a staple gun (see diagram left). You will have to use the paper glue in only two places, where the material is cut and tucked under at the Formica ends.

3 Screw the top-fixing curtain rod tightly up behind the fascia. Only the runners should appear below the fascia (see below).

4 Staple the stiff side of the Velcro onto the returns of the board only.

5 Have the board fixed securely to the wall above the window (see page 40). Hand sew a strip of soft Velcro to the last 10cm (4in) of the outside edge of each curtain just below the top. This Velcro is stuck to that on the return of the board.

material. And when the curtains are closed, all is discreetly hidden, since the top of the curtain is level with the top of the board.

I feel that only French- and goblet-pleated curtains are suitable for this treatment, and French pleats are preferable because they stack up better when the curtains are open

The board and the fascia
The timber board that holds the top-fixing curtain rod must be 10cm (4in) deep and 2cm (¾in) thick. Determine the width of the board in the same way you calculate the width of a pelmet board (see **Table 2** on page 36).

Because something as thin as possible, yet also quite strong, is needed for the fascia, the only suitable material is Formica. You will need a piece about 5cm (2in) wide and 14cm (5½in) shorter than the board itself. Before cutting the Formica, read the instructions for making the board with fascia. Then check what the depth and width of the fascia must be for your particular rod. The fascia needs to cover the rod and allow only the runners to be visible under it.

When making the board with the covered fascia, you will need the following materials:

– The board
– The Formica fascia
– Wood glue and strong paper glue
– A curtain rod
– 20cm (8in) of 2cm (¾in)-wide Velcro
– Brackets to attach board to wall
– A remnant of curtain material adequate to cover the board

Measuring the curtain drop
One important thing to remember when using this type of board and fascia is that the finished curtain

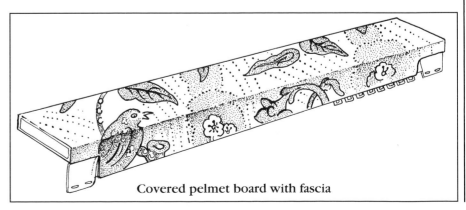

Covered pelmet board with fascia

Insert the pin hooks so that the top of the curtain will be level with the top of the board; then hang the curtains (see page 53 for hanging and dressing instructions).

CURTAINS ON A BRASS SWING ARM

Using brass swing arms for curtains is the most wonderful method of curtaining an eave, dormer or attic window. In such restricted spaces this is the only window treatment that will ensure that you do not lose one bit of light. To open the curtains you swing the arms back completely clear of the window.

Because you will see one side of the curtain when the curtains are opened and the other side when they are in front of the window, curtain material must be used for both sides; thus no lining is required. The ornamental focus of the top of the window treatment is a pretty stand-up along the top of the swing arm. To make this type of curtain even more attractive, always use tie-backs. They give the curtains a lovely shape.

Single swing arm over door
Another effective way of using brass swing arms is to hang a curtain off a single arm to cover a door leading outdoors. This works especially well if there is an adjacent wall beside the door, along which the opened brass arm can lie.

This treatment for a door has two marvellous advantages – it insulates the house against draughts and it creates a very decorative look for a relatively unexciting feature. Also, this curtain can be removed with the greatest ease in summertime.

The brass swing arms
Be sure to choose a swing arm of a good quality and one that you will be able to live with for a long time. You want to choose a fairly stylish brass swing arm (see *Suppliers* on page 128).

Curtains hanging from brass swing arms (left) are the perfect window treatment for an eave, dormer or attic window. None of the available incoming light is lost when this type of curtain is used.

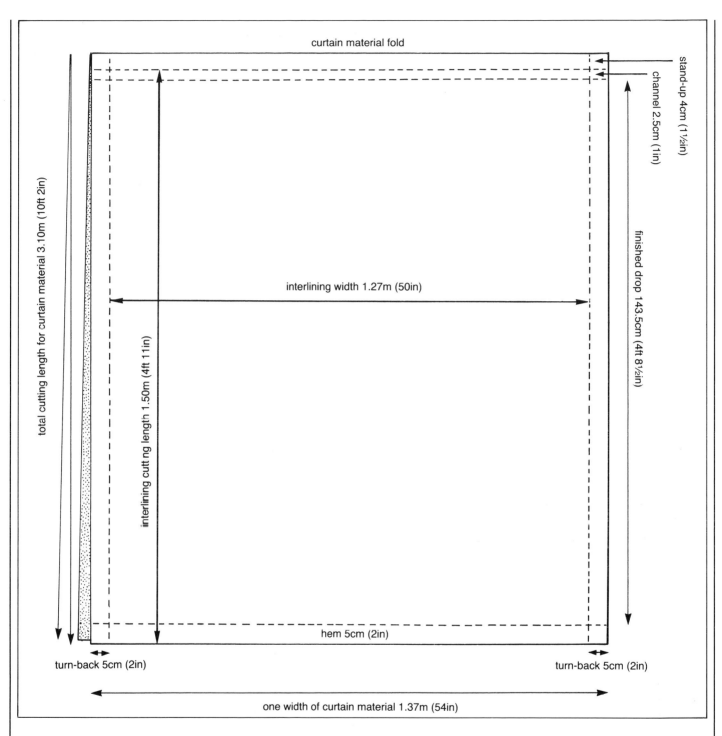

curtain material fold

stand-up 4cm (1½in)

channel 2.5cm (1in)

finished drop 143.5cm (4ft 8½in)

total cutting length for curtain material 3.10m (10ft 2in)

interlining width 1.27m (50in)

interlining cutting length 1.50m (4ft 11in)

hem 5cm (2in)

turn-back 5cm (2in)

turn-back 5cm (2in)

one width of curtain material 1.37m (54in)

To determine the length of the arm, measure the exact recess space in your eave or dormer window. Each swing arm sits in its own bracket, and they should come together in the centre, just touching when closed.

Total cutting length
You will want the swing arm level with the top of the window, so when measuring the drop, measure from this point. The finished length for this treatment is usually short, with the curtains either reaching the sill or extending just below it.

To determine the cutting length for the curtain material add the following:

– Curtain drop
– Hem of 5cm (2in)
– Casing for swing arm 2.5cm (1in)
– Stand-up 4cm (1½in)

In the diagram above, a sample curtain is given as the example for making curtains for a swing arm. You can see that the curtain material is folded in half along the top so that it will form both sides of the finished curtain. The length of one side of the curtain – including the finished drop, the hem, the casing for the swing arm and the stand-up – is 1.55m (5ft 1in). So the *total cutting length* for one curtain will be double this or 3.10m (10ft 2in). Be sure to use a print which has no 'top' or 'bottom'.

Finished flat curtain width

The width of each finished flat curtain for a swing arm should be about 2 times the length of the arm. The length of the arm for our sample curtain is 55cm (21¾in), so one width of curtain material 137cm (54in) wide is fine. A wider fabric would be too wide for the arm and would have to be trimmed back to 137cm (54in).

You will rarely have a swing arm long enough to require more than one width of curtain material, so there is no need to pattern-match.

Cutting the interlining

The curtains for a swing arm should be interlined, but the interlining does not need to be interlocked to the curtain. The dimensions of the interlining, in relation to the curtain material, are shown on the diagram on page 69. The interlining is 10cm (4in) narrower than the curtain material, and it is cut 5cm (2in) shorter than *half* of the total cutting length of the curtain.

Unlike for ordinary curtains, the interlining is not folded in along the sides of the curtains; instead, its raw edge ends at the edge of the finished curtain. There is no stress or friction on the vertical edges of this curtain since it is neither drawn by hand nor pulled backwards and forwards on a rod. So, because they are static, it is perfectly adequate simply to fold the curtain material over the flat interlining.

Sewing in the interlining

1 Cut the curtain material to the required length (see *Total cutting length* on page 69). Cut the interlining 5cm (2in) shorter than half of the total cutting length (see diagram on page 69).

2 Fold the length of curtain material in half width-wise, with wrong sides facing. Press in the fold to create a sharp line along what will be the edge of the stand-up.

3 Open out the curtain material and clamp it to the table, right side down, with the sharply pressed fold line along one end of the table and one selvedge running along the long edge of the table.

4 Place the interlining on top of the wrong side of the curtain material so that the top of the interlining lies 5cm (2in) below the fold line and the side edge is 5cm (2in) from the side edge of the curtain material. Smooth the interlining out gently, and pin its top edge to the curtain material.

5 Once the interlining is in place, remove the clamps. Fold the 5cm (2in) of curtain material that extends past the side edge of the interlining over the interlining, and again clamp the edge of the curtain to the table. Stitch the turned-back edge in place as for step 4 of *Turning back side edges of curtain* on page 46, but work the stitches from the very top edge of the interlining to within 12cm (4¾in) of the bottom.

6 Stitch along the other side edge of the curtain in the same way.

7 Now stitch the hem. Fold up 5cm (2in) of curtain material and interlining together and pin along the bottom, leaving the corners open. Then trim the interlining at the corners and form the corners following steps 4, 5 and 6 of *Hemming the curtain* on page 47. Fold the hem up again and pin the diagonal of the corner, without pinning it to the curtain directly below. Sew in a 3cm (1⅛in) lead weight, placing it under the diagonal fold. Then fold the corner back over it and pin. Make the second corner in the same way, then slipstitch the hem in place, beginning with the diagonal at the corner. Remove all of the pins.

8 With a short ruler, measure down 6.5cm (2½in) from the fold line at the top of the curtain, and mark the interlining with a pencil. Make marks at intervals along the top of the curtain the same distance from the fold line. Then draw a line to join the marks, using the long folding ruler as a guide. Leave the pins in the top of the interlining.

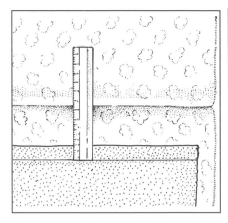

9 Machine stitch along the line to join the interlining to the single layer of curtain material below, stitching from one side edge to the other. The interlining is now firmly secured to the curtain material. Remove the pins and trim the excess interlining close to the stitches.

Making the heading

1 With the interlining facing upwards, bring the other side of the curtain material over to enclose it, folding the top again along the pressed fold line. Then fold under all 3 raw edges of the top layer so that they are level with the finished edges. Hand sew around 3 edges.

2 Turn the curtain over so that the side with the machine stitching is facing upwards. Mark a line 2.5cm (1in) above the machine line. Now machine stitch first on top of the existing line of stitches and then along the newly marked line. By doing this you have created a casing for the swing arm, as well as a 4cm (1½in) stand-up above it. Make the second curtain in the same way.

3 Feed each curtain onto a swing arm, and screw the swing arm stopper back on. Work one stitch at the end of the channel to tighten it. Then slot the swing arm back into the bracket. If the swing arm is rather long – say about a metre (yard) – or if the curtains are very heavy, use a receiver hook (an ordinary brass cup hook is fine) to take the weight off the arm when it is either open or closed. You will, however, rarely need to do this, as it is unusual for a swing arm to be this long or the curtains this heavy.

Chapter Six
CREATING PELMETS

Wherever it is possible, I like to include a pelmet in my window treatment. It 'crowns' and finishes off the window with such style, however simple or elaborate it is. This chapter gives instructions for making both straight-edged and curved-edge pelmets. Because the secret of a perfect pelmet is in its proportions, I include many tips on how you can achieve the right proportions in your pelmet. A successful pelmet is one that looks balanced in relation to the rest of the room.

Choosing a pelmet style

There are many types of pelmet to choose from. You should make your choice following the advice given in Chapter 1 about designing window treatments. Here I give instructions of eight types of straight-edged pelmet:

– Pencil pleated
– French pleated
– Goblet pleated
– Smocked-headed
– Velcro-headed with stand-up
– Gathered off a band
– Box-pleated
– Diamond-buttoned

The other four pelmets covered have a curved edge and include:

– Caught-up
– Soft continuous curves
– Single continuous curve or arched
– Serpent tail

Whatever pelmet style you choose, be sure to take great care in deciding on the finished drop.

Perfect proportions

I see the window as a 'face' and the pelmet as its 'hat'; if the 'hat' is too small for the 'face', it will remind one of a great fat face with a beret that is far too small perched on top. This has the effect of broadening the face all the more. Equally, if the 'face' is long and thin and the hat is similar in proportion (especially if it has deep fringing on its lower edge), then the 'face' will look as if it cannot see out.

There are many different theories on pelmet proportions and I, of course, strongly believe in my own: for every 30cm (12in) of drop of curtain allow 5cm (2in) for the drop of the pelmet. I stress that this is merely a guide and not a rule, since there are so many variables to consider:

– Direction the window is facing
– Nature of material
– Position of pelmet board
– Straight or curved edge of pelmet

What is helpful (a Jean Monro tip) is to get someone else to hold your 2m (6ft) ruler up against the window with a handkerchief tied around it at the point where you want the pelmet to drop.

Finished pleated width of pelmet

The finished pleated width of the pelmet corresponds, of course, to the 'total width' of the pelmet board. When the 'total width' of the board is mentioned in relation to a pelmet, it always includes the returns, since the pelmet must cover the entire edge of the board.

The sample board shown in the illustration below is the size of the board used in many of the pelmet instructions that follow.

Perfect fullness

In general, pelmets should be fuller than curtains. Most of the pelmets that I give instructions for look best with a fullness of about 3 to 3½ times the total pelmet board measurement.

When deciding how many widths of material you will need for your pelmets, multiply the total width of the board by 3. Then determine how many widths of your chosen material you will need. Try not to use half widths, if possible, since it would mean splitting that half width in half again to place a quarter width at each end of the pelmet. If in doubt, go for a slightly fuller pelmet. You do have the option of making the pelmet only 2½ times the width of the board if you do not want a really full pelmet, but to my mind it is much more attractive if it has more fullness than your curtains.

When following the instructions given for the sample pelmets, there is no need to worry about whether the material being used is 120cm (48in) wide or 137cm (54in). This is because the fullness of 3 to 3½ times the total board width is broad enough to cover these small discrepancies.

The three exceptions to this rule for fullness are the smocked-headed pelmet, the soft continuous-curves pelmet and the diamond-buttoned pelmet. They all require less fullness. The instructions for each of these styles show how to achieve perfect fullness in each instance.

Cutting length for pelmet widths

As for curtains, the cutting length for each width of pelmet material is determined by adding together the following:

– Finished pelmet drop
– Allowance for hem
– Turn-down at top

The allowances for the hem and the turn-down depend on the type of pelmet you are making, and the measurements are given in the instructions of the individual pelmets.

Pelmet trimmings

Ready-made trimmings or hand-made frills (see page 20) can be added to most types of pelmet, whether it is straight-edged or has a curved edge. When calculating the finished drop of the pelmet, remember to add the length of the trimming.

Calculating material amounts

When calculating how much length to allow for each width of material used in the pelmet, you must add the length of the pattern repeat (unless you are using a plain material). This means that the drop

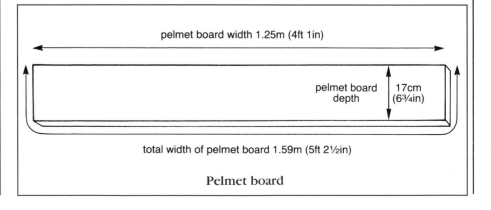

pelmet board width 1.25m (4ft 1in)

pelmet board depth   17cm (6¾in)

total width of pelmet board 1.59m (5ft 2½in)

Pelmet board

allowance for each width, as for curtains, is the cutting length plus the pattern repeat.

Do not forget to add the amount needed for any handmade frill or piping when determining how much material you need.

Joining the widths
As for curtains, the widths will have to be pattern-matched when they are joined together (see page 44).

If you are joining an odd number of widths, you can simply join them one after another. However, if your pelmet requires an even number of widths you will not be able to do this because you should never have a seam running up the centre of a pelmet. So, when joining an even number of widths, cut one of the widths in half and place it at either end of the pelmet.

Lining and interlining amounts
Because there is no need for pattern-matching, you will need less lining and interlining than pelmet material. But you must take into account the width from selvedge to selvedge of the lining and inter-lining. It may not match the width of the pelmet material, and you will have to compensate for this when joining the widths.

I nearly always interline pelmets (with a medium-weight interlining). Not only do they look and hang much better, but the sun will not reveal those endless turnings and bulky seams of inset frills.

Attaching the pelmet to the board
All pelmets are attached to the board with 2cm (¾in)-wide Velcro. The soft side of the Velcro is sewn to the back of the pelmet; and the stiff side is stapled to the front and return edges of the board.

PENCIL-PLEATED PELMET
The pencil-pleated pelmet is one of the simplest to make. It has a soft, informal appearance and is quick and easy to put together.

Perfect proportions
I use a pencil-pleat tape 8cm (3¼in) wide for pelmets whose drop is between 25cm and 35cm (10in and

13¾in). On deeper pelmets I would use a 14.5cm (5¾in)-deep tape, since the narrower tape would look too insignificant. Generally I think a pencil-pleated pelmet can have a drop of up to about 60cm (24in).

The sample pelmet
The pelmet used as the example in the instructions has a finished drop of 30cm (12in) and a finished width (including returns) of 1.59m (5ft 2½in). The pencil-pleat tape being used is 8cm (3½in) wide; however, the techniques used would be the same for a deeper tape.

The cutting length for the material is determined by adding to the finished drop:

– A hem allowance of 5.5cm (2in)
– A turn-down at the top of 5cm (2in)

That makes the cutting length for the sample pelmet 40.5cm (16in).

The cutting length for the lining for this type of pelmet is 2.5cm (1in) less than the finished drop, or 27.5cm (11in) for the sample pelmet. The interlining should be cut the exact length of the finished drop.

The recommended fullness for a pencil-pleated pelmet is about 3 to 3 ½ times the total width of the board, so 4 widths are needed for the sample pelmet.

Cutting and joining the widths
Cut and join the material widths, pattern-matching as you did for your curtains. Cut the lining and the interlining the lengths required, and join them to make the same overall width as the pelmet material. (The lining is not hemmed in the way curtain lining is hemmed.)

Making the pelmet
1 Placing right sides and raw edges together, machine stitch the lower edge of the pelmet material to the lower edge of the lining 1.5cm (½in) from the edge. Press to embed the stitches, then press the seam open.

2 Fold the pelmet material wrong sides together along the width of the material 4cm (1½in) below the

seam just stitched and press, measuring as you go. This creates a 4cm (1½in) hem of pelmet material on the wrong side. The top edge of the lining will now be 5cm (2in) below the top of the pelmet material.

3 With the pelmet wrong side up, turn down 5cm (2in) of pelmet material along the top, over the lining; press. The pelmet should now measure 30cm (12in), the finished drop, from top to bottom.

4 Insert the interlining between the pelmet material and the lining so that it fits exactly between the pressed-up hem and the pressed-down turning at the top. Trim 4cm (1½in) off both side edges of the interlining only.

5 Pin the turn-down in place, inserting the pins vertically so that the pinheads stick up above the top edge of the curtain.

6 At the unfinished side edges, fold 4cm (1½in) of the lining and the pelmet material to the inside (between the lining and the interlining), and pin. Slipstitch the lining to the pelmet material to finish the side edges.

7 Machine stitch the tape to the heading and gather the pelmet as for making the pencil-pleat heading for curtains (see steps 5 and 6 on page 49).

8 Check again that the finished width of the pelmet is correct. The soft side of the Velcro is now sewn to the back of the pelmet. The top edge of the Velcro should be level

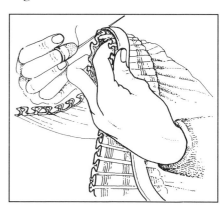

with the top edge of the pelmet. Sew the Velcro along the top edge first, bending the heading around your fingers as you sew (see diagram on page 73) so that the pelmet does not 'shrink' as the Velcro is stitched to it. After sewing the top edge of the Velcro, sew along the bottom edge.

FRENCH- AND GOBLET-PLEATED PELMETS

French pleats are possibly a little more interesting than pencil pleats and have a more tailored look. Goblet pleats are made in almost exactly the same way but their final appearance is distinctly different. In my opinion they have a slightly grander look than French pleats.

Perfect proportions

It is essential that the depth of the pleats not be too heavy for the drop of the pelmet. The depth of the pleats (and the fusible buckram) should be about one-third of the finished drop for both French and goblet pleats. In terms of maximum drop, these pleats look good on a drop of up to 60cm (24in).

The sample pelmet

The pelmet used as the example in the instructions that follow has a finished drop of 30cm (12in) and a finished width of 1.59m (5ft 2½in). The pleats (and therefore the fusible buckram) are 10cm (4in) deep.

The cutting length for the material for a French- or goblet-pleated pelmet is determined by adding to the finished drop:

– A hem allowance of 5.5cm (2in)
– A turn-down at the top 3cm (1¼in) more than depth of the fusible buckram

For the sample pelmet this would mean adding a turn-down of 13cm (5¼in), which makes the cutting length 48.5cm (19¼in).

The cutting length for the lining and the interlining is the same as for

The very slightly curved shape (see page 85 for single continuous-curve pelmets) of the pencil-pleated pelmet (left) is accentuated by the pretty contrast-bound inset frill.

the pencil-pleated pelmet.

The recommended fullness for French- and goblet-pleated pelmets is 3 times the total width of the board, so 4 widths are needed for the sample pelmet.

Making the pelmet

1 Cut and join the widths as for the pencil-pleated pelmet.

2 Follow steps 1 and 2 of making the pencil-pleated pelmet, but note that when step 2 has been completed, the top of the lining will be 13cm (5¼in) below the top of the pelmet material.

3 Insert the interlining between the pelmet material and the lining so that it fits from the fold line of the pressed-up hem to the top of the lining. Trim 4cm (1½in) off both side edges of the interlining only.

4 Keeping the excess pelmet material at the top opened out, fold under and slipstitch the side edges as in step 6 of the pencil-pleated pelmet.

5 Complete the heading as for making the French-pleat curtain heading steps 3–6 on page 73, but note that in step 3 the lining is already stitched to the top edge and that in step 6 the turn-down for the pelmet is 13cm (5¼in).

6 Calculate for the pleats as for the French-pleated curtains, then make the pleats as for the curtains (omitting the curtain hooks).

7 Sew Velcro to the top of the pelmet as for the pencil-pleated pelmet.

SMOCKED-HEADED PELMET

Smocking is one of my favourite designs for a pelmet heading. Although it looks quite complicated, it is actually simple and painless to achieve – which makes it very satisfying! This type of pelmet is especially suitable for a bedroom, but there is no reason why it should not be used in a reception room.

It is essential when making a smocked-headed pelmet to use only the best-quality smocking tape. An

inferior tape will not pull up properly and the results will not be nearly so good.

The smocking stitches are worked onto the front of the heading after the flat pelmet has been finished and the smocking tape stitched to the back. Six strands of stranded cotton embroidery floss are used for the smocking. You can use a matching thread, but a contrast looks much more effective.

Perfect proportions and fullness

A smocked-headed pelmet, using the classic smoking tape, can be made with a drop of between 25cm and 45cm (10in and 17¾in).

For perfect fullness, however, the finished flat width of the pelmet before smocking must be twice the total width of the board and no more. This is important because otherwise the diamond shapes will not be pulled apart sufficiently.

The sample pelmet

The sample pelmet is the same as for the pencil-pleated pelmet. The smocked-headed pelmet is made exactly as for the pencil-pleated pelmet except that the finished flat width of the pelmet must be exactly 3.18m (10ft 5in), so you will probably need only 3 widths of material, which will then be trimmed at each side after the widths are joined to achieve the correct finished width. When trimming, remember to leave a 4cm (1½in) turn-back allowance at each side.

Follow all the steps for making the pencil-pleated pelmet, but, of course, machine stitch an 8.5cm (3¼in)-wide smocking tape to the heading instead of pencil-pleat tape, and do not sew on the Velcro until the smocking is complete. Note that the smocking tape has 4 cords and must be sewn on with the hook pockets facing upwards or the diamonds will not form correctly.

Honeycomb smocking stitches

1 Once the tape has been gathered up to the correct finished width, you can smock the heading.

2 Thread a large needle with 6 strands of embroidery floss and knot

the end. With the right side of the pelmet facing you and working from left to right, pinch the first two pleats at the left together. Pass the

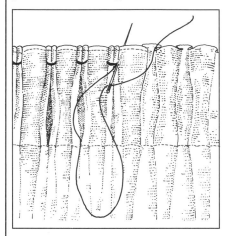

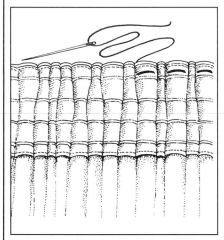

needle from back to front, bringing it out 5mm (¼in) to the left of the first pleat fold and 1cm (⅜in) from the top of the pelmet. Then insert the needle from right to left through the first 2 pleats, 5mm (¼in) to the right side of the 2nd pleat fold and out at the starting point. Then insert it again through the 2nd pleat at the same point it was inserted before but this time pass the needle through the pelmet and out the back. Repeat this process for every pair of pleats across the heading at the same level. The diagrams above show the front and back of the heading as the first row of stitches are being worked.

3 Now repeat the process, but along the bottom of the tape directly over the machine stitching, sewing the same pairs of pleats together. Do not be discouraged about how

untidy the heading looks at this stage; you will be arranging the pleats properly later.

4 Repeat the same process along the middle of the tape (see below), but this time start by sewing the 2nd and 3rd pleat together instead of the first and 2nd, to create the lovely diamond shapes.

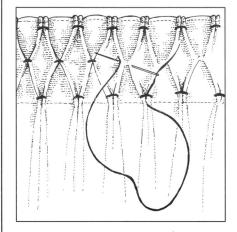

5 Sew on the Velcro as for the pencil-pleated pelmet.

VELCRO-HEADED PELMET WITH A STAND-UP

I love a 'stand-up' along the top of a pelmet. It makes the pelmet look perfectly balanced when it is hanging in place. All pelmets hang down, so why not have a part of them going up as well?

Like the Velcro-headed curtains (page 64), this pelmet has a plaited or ruched band hand sewn over the gathers.

Perfect proportions and fullness
The recommended fullness for a Velcro-headed pelmet with a stand-up is about 3 times the total width of the board.

Making the pelmet
This pelmet is made without interlining. Follow the instructions for the Velcro-headed curtains (see page 64) to make the pelmet.

GATHERED PELMET WITH BAND

The gathered pelmet with a fusible-buckram band has a lovely old-fashioned look about it. This type of pelmet was traditionally to be found hanging from the canopies and

bases of imposing four-poster beds.

A gathered pelmet with band must be hung from a pelmet board with a plywood fascia (page 39).

Perfect proportions
The depth of the band should be about one-third of the finished drop of the pelmet, so that the remaining two-thirds consist of the skirt. The longest you could make this pelmet would be 50cm (20in), allowing for a buckram band of 15cm (6in) and a skirt of 35cm (14in).

Perfect fullness
The fusible-buckram band on this pelmet is, of course, the exact measurement of the total pelmet-board width, but the gathered skirt should be about 2½ to 3 times this measurement. To ensure a light appearance, the skirt is usually not interlined, although the buckram band is. (If interlining is required for the gathered skirt, only a lightweight interlining, or domette, should be used.)

The sample pelmet
The sample pelmet has a finished drop of 30cm (12in) and a total finished width of 1.59cm (5ft 2½in). The buckram-stiffened band is 10cm (4in) deep, and the skirt has a 20cm (8in) finished drop.

The cutting length for the skirt material is determined by adding to the finished drop of the skirt:

– A hem allowance of 5.5cm (2in)
– A seam allowance at the top of 1.5cm (½in)

This makes the cutting length for the sample skirt 27cm (10½in). The lining for the skirt has a cutting length 1cm (½in) shorter than the finished drop, which gives 19cm (7½in) for the sample pelmet. The sample pelmet skirt requires 4 widths of material.

The band piece has a seam allowance, top and bottom, of 1.5cm (½in); and should have a turn-back

Although this pelmet (right) has an excellent contrast-bound French-pleat heading, the window treatment would have been much improved if the curtains had been interlined.

allowance at each end of 4cm (1½in). So for a 10cm (4in) band you will need to cut the band material 13cm (5in) deep and 1.67m (5ft 5½in) long. The lining should be cut exactly the same size as the band material. The interlining for the band should be cut to the width of the finished band – in this case 10cm (4in) – and the same length as the band material and lining.

Cutting and joining the widths
Cut and join the widths as explained for the pencil-pleated pelmet.

Covering the piping cord
1 Both the top and bottom of the band are edged with piping cord. The cord is best covered in a contrasting colour. Cut 2 pieces of piping cord, each the total length of the pelmet board. Then cut strips of material on the bias, wide enough to cover the cord and allowing for a 1.5cm (½in) seam allowance on both edges; a width of about 4cm (1½in) should be sufficient. Cut enough strips to cover both cords.

2 Machine stitch the strips together to make a cover for each cord, allowing an extra 1.5cm (½in) at each end. Press the seams on the strips open.

3 Fold in 1.5cm (½in) at the beginning and end of one strip and press. Lay the cord in the centre of the wrong side of the strip with the ends tucked under the turn-backs. Fold the strip over the cord, matching the raw edges. (Always use the zipper foot when stitching close to the cord.) Machine stitch close to the cord. Cover the other cord in the same way.

Making the pelmet
1 Placing right sides and raw edges together, machine stitch the covered piping cord to the top of the band material 1.5cm (½in) from the edge (close to the cord), first positioning the cord so that it begins and ends

A lovely fan edging has been used to trim the serpent shape of this pelmet with a gathered skirt off a buckram-interfaced band (left). The edging is echoed on the roller blind.

4cm (1½in) from each side edge. Sew the other cord to the bottom of the band in the same way.

2 Placing right sides and raw edges together, machine stitch the band lining and material together along the top 1.5cm (½in) from the edge.

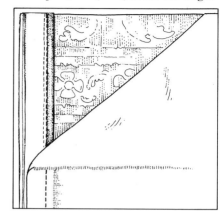

3 Cut a piece of soft 2cm (¾in)-wide Velcro the exact total width of the pelmet board. Now machine stitch the Velcro to the very top of the right side of the lining only,

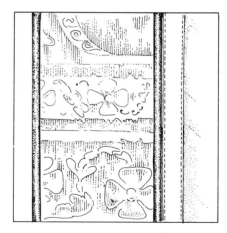

as close to the covered cord as possible and all around the Velcro. The Velcro is 4cm (1½in) shorter than the lining at each end to allow for turn-backs.

4 With the right sides and the raw edges together, machine stitch the lower edge of the skirt material to the lower edge of the lining 1.5cm (½in) from the edge. Press to embed the stitches, then press the seam open. Fold the lining and the skirt material wrong sides together, so that the top raw edges are level, and press the hemline fold. Turn in 2cm (¾in) at the side edges and

slipstitch the lining to the skirt material. Press. Machine stitch along the top edge of the skirt 1.5cm (½in) from the raw edge through both skirt and lining. Then machine gather the skirt to measure the total width of the pelmet board (see page 21 for machine gathering).

5 Now, placing right sides and raw edges together, machine stitch the finished skirt to the lower edge of the band material 1.5cm (½in) from the edge. Trim the seam. Then fold 4cm (1½in) to the wrong side along the band material and lining at the side edges; press.

6 Trim 4cm (1½in) off each end of the strip of interlining and insert it between the band material and the lining. Then insert a strip of fusible buckram exactly the same size as the

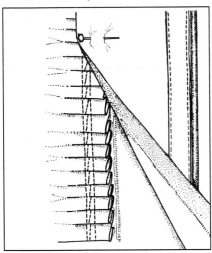

interlining on top of the interlining. Pull the lining tightly over the back of the band to cover the buckram, turn under the lower edge just below the raw edge of the gathered skirt; pin. Slipstitch the lining in place. Press the back of the band so that the heat will glue in the fusible buckram.

BOX-PLEATED PELMET WITH BAND

The box-pleated pelmet with a fusible-buckram band is another beautiful pelmet design and, again, rather old-fashioned in style. It is made in much the same way as the gathered pelmet with a band. However, it is more time-consuming to make, since you must measure

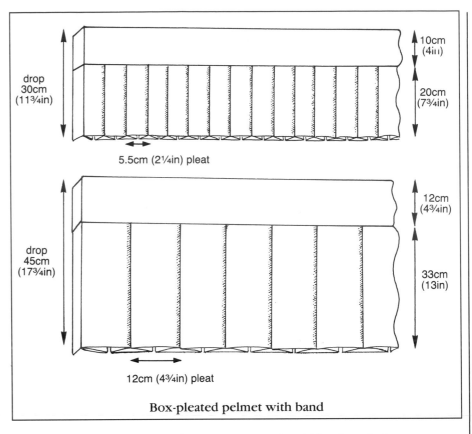

drop 30cm (11¾in) | 10cm (4in) | 20cm (7¾in) | 5.5cm (2¼in) pleat

drop 45cm (17¾in) | 12cm (4¾in) | 33cm (13in) | 12cm (4¾in) pleat

Box-pleated pelmet with band

the pleats. The skirt of the pelmet is not interlined; this allows the pleats to hang properly.

Perfect proportions
The perfect proportions for this pelmet are the same as for the gathered pelmet with a band. The width of the pleats depends on the drop of the pelmet. The longer the drop, the wider the pleats should be to balance their length (see the illustration above).

Perfect fullness
Again the fusible-buckram band on this pelmet is the exact length of the pelmet board.

Unlike the pelmet with the gathered skirt, however, the fullness cannot be so approximate. Whenever pleats are involved you will have to make your calculations more accurately. For box pleats, of any width, with no gaps between the pleats (either on the right side or the wrong side) the finished flat skirt must be approximately 3 times the total length of the board. If there are gaps between the pleats the width will have to be less than this. Calculating for pleats is not difficult,

but should be done before you start making your pelmet.

Making the pelmet
Make the pelmet as for the gathered pelmet with a band, but make the skirt the required finished width and form the pleats as required.

DIAMOND-BUTTONED PELMET
The diamond-buttoned pelmet is not only an extremely attractive design for a pelmet, it is also highly versatile (see left). You can vary its proportions considerably to suit the style of the room. This design came about when a pelmet with a very shallow drop was required – such as 15cm (6in). Such a short drop would obviously rule out all of the pelmet styles described so far, with the possible exception of the Velcro-headed pelmet with a stand-up. This versatility makes the diamond-buttoned pelmet a very useful design.

As for a box-pleated pelmet, the pleats here should not be interlined.

Perfect proportions and fullness
The thing to remember is that the longer the drop of the pelmet, the

The box pleats on this pelmet (above) are nice and wide which gives them a pleasing boldness (see proportions for box pleats on facing page).

wider the pleats should be.

As for all box pleats, the finished flat width of the pelmet must be carefully calculated before the material is cut. The same principle applies as for the skirt of the box-pleated pelmet.

The sample pelmet
The sample diamond-buttoned pelmet used in the instructions that follow has a finished drop of 20cm (8in) and a total finished width of 1.39m (4ft 6½in).

The cutting length for the pelmet material is determined by adding to the finished drop:

– A hem allowance of 5.5cm (2in)
– A turn-down at the top of 6.5cm (2½in)

For the sample pelmet this would mean a cutting length of 32cm (12½in).

The cutting length of the lining is 6cm (2½in) less than the finished drop, or 14cm (5½in) for the sample pelmet.

Because the sample pelmet has gaps between the pleats and no

pleats along the returns, the finished flat width is less than twice the total pelmet-board width. After joining, the pelmet material should be 2.69m (8ft 9¼in), which allows 2cm (¾in) to be turned under at each side. This means that 2 widths of a 137cm (54in)-wide material will be sufficient. The width of the lining is the same as for the pelmet material.

Cutting and joining the widths
Cut and join the widths as instructed for the pencil-pleated pelmet.

Making the pelmet
1 Placing right sides and raw edges together, machine stitch the pelmet material to the lining at both top and bottom, 1.5cm (½in) from the edge to form a tube. Press to embed the stitches.

2 Turn the tube right side out and adjust the seams so that you end up with a 4cm (1½in) hem and a 5cm (2in) turn-down at the top. Press.

3 Fold 2cm (¾in) to the inside at the sides and slipstitch. Press. The finished flat width now measures 2.65m (8ft 7¾in).

4 Now place the pelmet right side upwards, and mark the positions of the pleats across the heading, inserting the pins vertically so that the pinheads stick up above the top edge. First mark the positions of the returns, 17cm (6¾in) from each end. The gaps and pleats are marked out between these 2 pins. Beginning and ending with a gap, mark for a

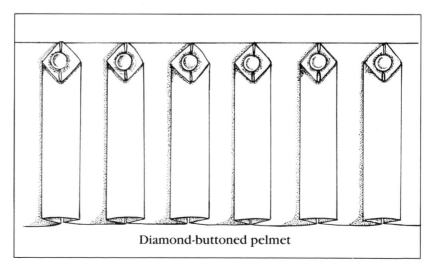

Diamond-buttoned pelmet

gap and a pleat alternately. Each of the 15 gaps across the heading measures 7cm (2¾in) and each of the 14 spaces for the box pleats measures 9cm (3½in).

5 Placing wrong sides together, bring together two pins at either side of each 9cm (3½in) space, and pin to form the pleats. Then machine stitch down each pleat approximately one-third the drop of the pelmet or, in this instance, 7cm (2¾in). See *Making French pleats* on curtains step 3, on page 59, for how to machine stitch the pleats across the heading.

6 Now, working from top to bottom, pin each pleat flat on the right side of the pelmet, placing the seam exactly in the middle. As you do this, measure at the top and the bottom of the pleat to check that it is correct. Press the pleats and remove the pins. Pull the front of each pleat down to form a diamond shape, and press.

7 Use a contrasting material to cover the 1.5cm (⅝in) buttons, and sew one to the centre of each diamond.

8 Sew the soft Velcro to the back as for the pencil-pleated pelmet (see page 73).

CAUGHT-UP PELMET

The caught-up pelmet is a sensational one – soft and natural and not at all regimented. It is extraordinarily easy to put together, but has the satisfying quality of appearing highly complicated and difficult to achieve. It is the perfect way to achieve a stunning window treatment when you want soft curves which look less tailored than swags and tails.

Perfect proportions and fullness
This pelmet is made in exactly the same way as the gathered pelmet with a band, and the same rule for fullness applies.

The proportions, however, are slightly different because the skirt is caught up; therefore the band should not be as deep as one-third of the total drop. This pelmet will not look good on a window whose drop is under 2.40m (8ft) or whose width is under 1.30m (4ft 4in).

The sample pelmet
The sample pelmet has curtains with a drop of 2.60m (8ft 7in) and a total pelmet-board width of 1.71m (5ft 7½in). The buckram band is 12cm (4¾in) deep.

The pelmet is made in exactly the same way as the gathered pelmet with a band. Then once the pelmet is hanging in place it is caught up at intervals as explained below.

Catching up the pelmet
1 Find the centre of the pelmet, and mark it with a pin on the lower piping line. This is point B on the diagram below. Then mark points A and C, equidistant from B as shown. These are the positions where the pelmet will be caught up.

2 Mark point E and D below point A. Pinch the material together at D and raise it up to point E, then pinch together the material at E and raise points D and E together to point A; pin. Using a strong matching thread, sew the folds in position with about 4 small stitches.

3 Catch up the skirt in the same way to points B and C.

4 Make 3 flower rosettes (see page 121) and sew one on top of each set of tucks.

SOFT CONTINUOUS-CURVES PELMET

The soft continuous-curves pelmet is especially beautiful in a bay window. The joy of it is that it works so well with so many different proportions and details, so you can make it as simple or elaborate as you like.

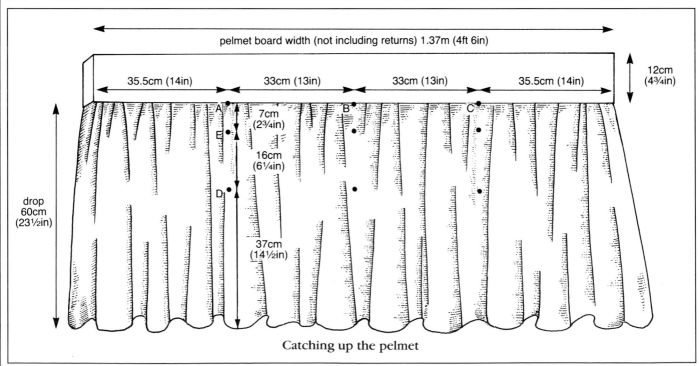

Catching up the pelmet

A wonderful contrast is produced in this window treatment (above) by the pattern running on the vertical on the box pleats and curtains, yet on the horizontal on the band.

You must always interline this pelmet. It is also essential that it have a trimming of some description along the lower edge. The trimming is needed to accentuate the lovely shape and rhythm of the continuous curves.

Perfect proportions
The shorter version of this pelmet should never have a finished drop of less than 20cm (8in) at the shortest point. The longest version I tend to make has a drop of 40cm (15¾in) at the shortest point. The longest point on the pelmet should be about 10cm (4in) more than the shortest in order to give it an attractive curve.

Perfect fullness
The perfect fullness for this pelmet is a finished flat width of 1½ times the total pelmet-board width, which makes it a very economical pelmet in terms of material. One French pleat is placed above the centre of the shallowest part of each curve to take up the excess material.

The sample pelmet
The sample pelmet is intended for curtains that have a drop of 2.70m (8ft 10½in). The total pelmet-board width is 2.20m (7ft 3in). The finished drop of the pelmet at the shortest point is 30cm (12in) and at the longest point, 40cm (15¾in). The pelmet has a handmade inset frill (see page 20).

The finished flat (or unpleated) width of the sample pelmet is 3.30m (11ft ¾in).

The pelmet material, lining and interlining are cut with the aid of a template. The top of the sample pelmet is interfaced with a fusible-buckram band 10cm (4in) deep.

Making the template
1 You can make your template out of newspaper (see page 85). Once you have determined the finished drop at the shortest and the longest points, you must decide how wide to make each curve. The sample pelmet has a curve 55cm (21⅝in) wide, so draw 2 vertical parallel lines this far apart.

2 Now draw a horizontal line across the top. For a buckram band 10cm (4in) wide you need a turn-down of 13cm (5in) at the top (see *French pleats*, page 57). Draw a horizontal line this distance below the first line to mark the position of the finished top of the pelmet.

3 Now mark the point of the longest drop at both sides of the template and the shortest drop at the centre of the template. Use a piece of piping cord as a guide in drawing the curve between these points. Then add a 1.5cm (½in) seam allowance along the bottom of the curve. Cut out the template.

Making the pelmet
1 The cutting length for the pelmet material is 54.5cm (21¼in). Cut and pattern-join enough widths to make up a width of 3.38m (11ft 3¾in). This is 8cm (3in) more than the finished flat width of the pelmet to allow for a 4cm (1½in) turn-back at each side edge.

2 The cutting length for the lining and the interlining is 13cm (5in) less than the pelmet material, or in this case 41.5cm (16¼in). Cut and join the lining and interlining to make up the same width as the pelmet material.

3 Use the template to mark the shape onto the pelmet material. Fold the material in half vertically, right sides together. Place the edge

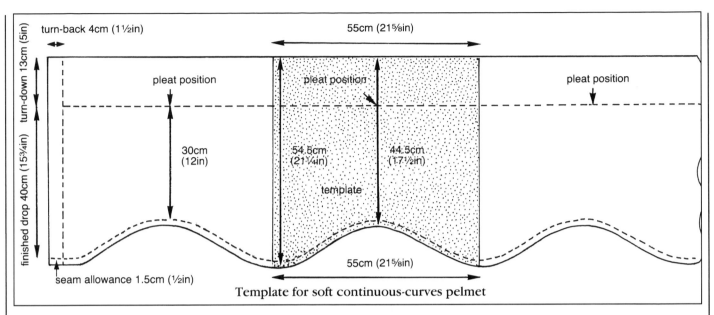

turn-back 4cm (1½in)

turn-down 13cm (5in)

55cm (21⅝in)

pleat position

pleat position

pleat position

finished drop 40cm (15¾in)

30cm (12in)

54.5cm (21¼in)

44.5cm (17½in)

template

seam allowance 1.5cm (½in)

55cm (21⅝in)

Template for soft continuous-curves pelmet

of the template on the centre fold; pin. Draw along the template curves. Then move the template along and repeat the process. Do this to the end of the material. Keeping the pelmet material folded in half, cut along the marked curved line.

4 Use the cut pelmet, opened out, as the template for the lining and the interlining.

5 Make the inset frill (see page 20) long enough to fit along the lower edge of the pelmet, and machine stitch it to the lower edge of the pelmet material as instructed in the inset-frill instructions.

6 Place the lining on the pelmet material with right sides facing, and pin them together very carefully along the lower edge. Place the interlining on top of the lining and pin along the same edge.

7 With the wrong side of the pelmet material facing upwards, machine stitch the layers together just inside the stitching used to attach the frill.

8 Trim the interlining close to the seam. Then trim the pelmet material, frill and lining seams to

Unlike the soft continuous curves in the illustration on the right, the curves of this pelmet (left) are slightly swagged. Also there are no French pleats across the heading.

5mm (¼in), and clip the seam allowance at intervals to ease the curve. Turn the pelmet right side out and press on the wrong side.

9 Trim 4cm (1½in) off the interlining at each end. Then fold 4cm (1½in) of the pelmet material and the lining to the inside and slipstitch the lining to the pelmet material.

10 Follow steps 5–7 of making the French-pleated pelmet, but making only one French pleat centred above the shortest part of each curve.

SINGLE CONTINUOUS-CURVE OR ARCHED PELMET

This pelmet exudes elegance if correctly cut and proportioned. It requires no template; the single continuous curve is merely marked

out with a series of dots or pins and then cut! The secret is to be bold when cutting and to understand the proportions of the pelmet in relation to the drop and width of the window.

It is essential to trim the lower edge of this pelmet with some sort of contrast, whether fringe or a handmade gathered frill. Without a trimming the pelmet loses much of its impact.

This pelmet is fairly extravagant on material since there is a lot of wastage in the central sections when cutting. However, it is likely that you will be using this wastage to make your frill or perhaps to make a tie-back, so do not worry!

Perfect fullness
A continuous curve will hang beautifully, provided it is fairly full.

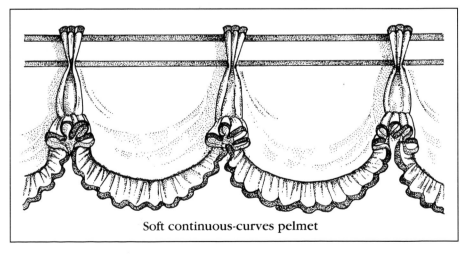

Soft continuous-curves pelmet

Therefore you should allow about 3 times the total width of the pelmet board if you are making a pencil-pleat, French- or goblet-pleat heading. You can use other headings, but make sure that you use the correct fullness for whichever heading you choose.

Perfect proportions

By far the best way to work out the proportions is to make a scale drawing on graph paper. Draw the whole window to scale with the curtains in place. Then, on a separate sheet, draw the pelmet to scale and cut it out. Then place it on top of the curtained window drawing to test the size (see the illustration right).

On a fairly tall and narrow window, for example 2.90m by 1.40m (9ft 7in by 4ft 7in), you should nearly always cut the pelmet so that the central drop is half the side drop at the end of the return. On a much wider window you will need to ease the sharpness of the curve.

The sample pelmet

The sample pelmet is shown in the diagram above. It has a finished centre drop of 40cm (15¾in) and a side drop of 80cm (2ft 7½in). The total width of the pelmet board is 1.74m (5ft 9in). It requires 4 widths of material. There is an inset frill along the lower edge, and it has a 14.5cm (5¾in)-deep pencil-pleat heading.

The cutting length for the pelmet material is determined by adding to the finished side drop:

– A seam allowance at the lower edge of 1.5cm (½in)
– A turn-down allowance at the top of 10cm (4in)

This makes the cutting length for the sample pelmet 91.5cm (3ft).

The lining and interlining are cut 10cm (4in) shorter, since they have no turn-down allowance. But note

Due to the immense height of the ceiling (left) and to the fact that the window receives a lot of light, the single continuous-curve pelmet in this window treatment is very deep.

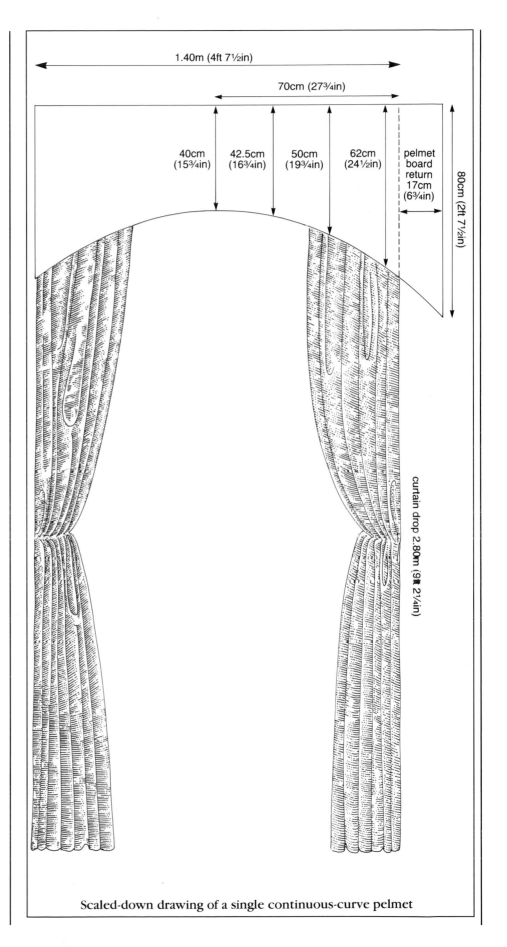

Scaled-down drawing of a single continuous-curve pelmet

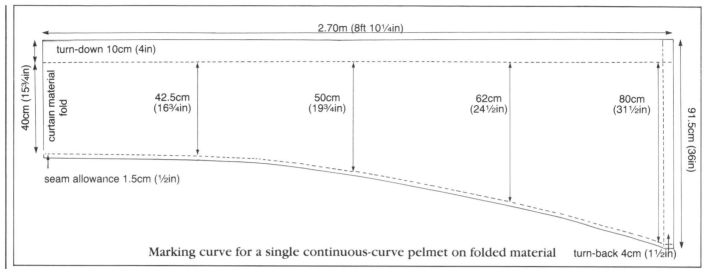

2.70m (8ft 10¼in)

turn-down 10cm (4in)

40cm (15¾in)

curtain material fold

42.5cm (16¾in)

50cm (19¾in)

62cm (24½in)

80cm (31½in)

91.5cm (36in)

seam allowance 1.5cm (½in)

Marking curve for a single continuous-curve pelmet on folded material   turn-back 4cm (1½in)

that when joining up the lining, you must use pelmet material for the last 40cm (15¾in) at both side edges. This is so that the lining will not show at the lower edge of the returns.

Cutting and joining the widths
1 Cut and join the widths as for the pencil-pleated pelmet.

2 Now fold the pelmet material in half, right sides together. Measure and mark the positions of the central drop, the drop at the side and 3 places equally spaced between (as shown above), taking the turn-down and the bottom seam allowance into account. Now lay a piping cord along these points to join them into a gradual curve. Ease the sharpness of the curve as it approaches the centre so that you do not end up with anything remotely resembling a V-shape at the centre – it should really be fairly flat at this point.

3 Having decided the shape, draw a line along the piping cord and cut! Your scissors must be absolutely

This single continuous-curve pelmet (right) is perfectly shaped for the low ceiling and wide windows. Two parallel lines of fan edging give the illusion of a set-on frill.

The strong contrast between the fringe and the pelmet material produces a serpent tail pelmet (facing page) with a powerful impact.

parallel with the top when you reach the centre and not pointing upwards.

4 Open out the pelmet material and use it as a template for the lining and interlining.

Making the pelmet
The pelmet is made up exactly as for the soft continuous-curves pelmet, except that the heading is made as for the pencil-pleated pelmet.

SERPENT-TAIL PELMET
The serpent-tail pelmet has such an attractive gently rhythmic shape. It looks equally good if the tail is cut either very long (half the overall drop of the curtains) or fairly short. The trick, as with the single continuous curve, is to cut the shape with great confidence. Again, it is an absolute necessity to have a trimming along the lower edge to accentuate the curve.

Perfect proportions and fullness
The fullness is the same as for the single continuous-curve pelmet. Bear in mind, when deciding on proportions, that LENGTH IS ELEGANCE where all window treatments are concerned, and this pelmet is no different. Decide on the finished drop for the centre, being generous on length since you are going to gain light from the two shorter parts of the pelmet. There must be a marked difference of at least 15cm (6in) between the drop in the centre and the drop at the two highest points (see right).

Decide the shape of the pelmet and make it in the same way as for the single continuous-curve pelmet.

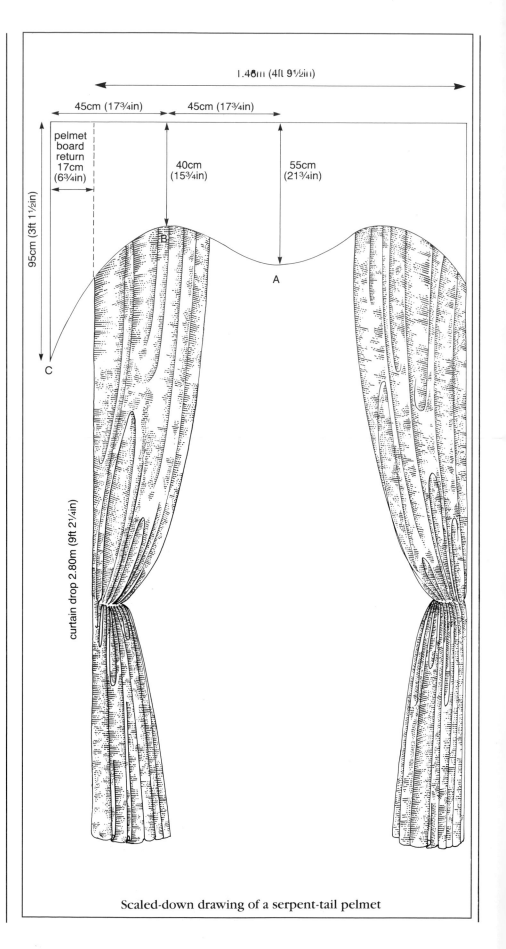

1.46m (4ft 9½in)

45cm (17¾in)   45cm (17¾in)

pelmet board return 17cm (6¾in)

40cm (15¾in)   55cm (21¾in)

95cm (3ft 11½in)

B

A

C

curtain drop 2.80m (9ft 2¼in)

Scaled-down drawing of a serpent-tail pelmet

Chapter Seven

SWAGS AND TAILS

In a class of their own, traditional swags and tails are probably the ultimate way to finish off your window treatment. To me they are the crown of all pelmets. Because the classic pleated swags are technically the most difficult type of pelmet to make, they would require a volume of their own to be properly explained. In this chapter, I present instead an alternative to the classic swags – ruched swags. These swags are a very effective and elegant substitute and are surprisingly easy to make.

TRADITIONAL SWAGS AND TAILS

The traditional swags and tails exude a serious elegance and indicate a certain awareness of the history of window treatments. It is the Georgian, Regency and even Victorian architectural proportions that best lend themselves to the design of this pelmet.

What makes the traditional swags so difficult to master technically is that they are pleated vertically. This requires a rather complicated template which must be made by experimentation with a piece of lining fabric.

RUCHED SWAGS AND TAILS

Ruched swags can be nearly as effective as the traditional version. Although their overall look is rather similar to that of traditional swags, their method of construction is totally different. Made from a single piece of curtain material, the ruched swags are vertically gathered to form their very pretty shape. The tails used with these swags, however, are identical to the traditional tails.

You should always use a trimming on ruched swags and tails, because it is the trimming which accentuates the shape and gives the treatment its final impact. Without trimming, this particular pelmet becomes a rather weak affair.

Perfect proportions

As with any pelmet design, it is essential to get the proportions of your swags and tails correct. The ruched swags can hang as far down the window as you are able to get away with, so long as they do not obscure too much light. They must also, of course, be in perfect balance with the size of your window and the proportions of your room.

I feel it is best to have a fairly decent drop in your window height if you want to use swags and tails, otherwise they look out of place. They will only work on a curtain drop of at least 2.40m (7ft 10¼in).

Both the pelmet and the curtains are a very good length for the overall design of these swags and tails (right) which have been finished off with choux rosettes.

Ruched swags and tails

When determining the length of the finished swags, remember that LENGTH IS ELEGANCE. In no situation is this more true than for swags. So, the longer you can make the swags, while retaining correct proportions, the better they will look. This goes for the tails as well. Their outside edges (near the wall) should be at least half the overall drop of the window. The inside edge of each tail looks extremely good if it has the same drop as the finished gathered swags at their longest point. However, this is definitely a question of taste.

Perfect fullness for the swags
Ruched swags have no gathers along their top edge they are the exact width of the pelmet board. The returns of the board are not taken into account here, because the swags cover only the front of the board, the returns being covered by tails.

The drop is where fullness is needed, because this is the direction of gathering. The finished swags, before gathering, need a drop double the finished lowest drop of the swag once gathered.

The difficulty with ruched swags is in deciding how many swags to have across a window. You will find that not all windows will be a suitable width for ruched swags. For two ruched swags, the width of your window treatment (or the pelmet board) should be about 1.10m–1.20m (3ft 7in–3ft 11in). If your pelmet board is about 50 per cent wider than this, or 1.50m–1.60m (4ft 11in–5ft 2in), you can then very successfully use three ruched swags across the window, and so on. In other words you can add one more swag for every 50cm–60cm (20in–24in), but any window treatment that does not allow for this will not be suitable for ruched swags. If you experiment with a piece of material you will find that if there are only 2 swags across a width of more than 1.20m (3ft 11in) they will not hang well since there will be too much flat width for the length of the swag; and 3 swags will be too many.

Perfect fullness for the tails
Because the tails are a 'dress' detail, fixed in position at the sides of the

pelmet, they can be the same width for almost any width of window. I generally use a finished width of about 90cm (35½in) for all of the tails I make.

The sample swags and tails
The curtain drop and the pelmet-board width used in the sample ruched swags and tails are as follows:

– Curtain drop 2.40m (7ft 10¼in)
– Width of board 1.20m (3ft 11¼in)

The suggested dimensions for the tails on this size window are:

– Finished tail length 1.20m (3ft 11¼in)
– Width of unpleated tail 87cm (34½in)

The suggested dimensions for the swags on this size window are:

– Width of finished swag 120cm (3ft 11¼in)
– Length of swag before gathering 90cm (2ft 11½in)
– Drop of gathered swag 45cm (1ft 5¾in)

This example should give you an idea of what the perfect proportions of the swags and tails should be for a specific window. As with other types of pelmet, it is advisable to do a scale drawing of the curtains on graph paper to test the dimensions you have decided on for the swags and tails (see page 87).

Making the ruched swags
1 Make the desired handmade frill (see page 20) or purchase a ready-made trimming such as fringing. For the swags you will need enough trimming to cover the width of the pelmet board (see *Tails* for length of trimming required for tails).

2 For the sample swags the finished lined and interlined swags should measure 90cm by 120cm (2ft 11½in

Well-dressed curtains will always en-hance a window treatment, whether it has swags and tails as here (right) or no pelmet at all (see page 53 for how to dress your curtains).

by 3ft 11¼in) before the rectangular piece is gathered horizontally (see diagram for step 7). So begin by cutting the swag material 93cm by 123cm (3ft ½in by 4ft ¼in). This will allow for 1.5cm (½in) seams. Be sure to cut the material so that the drop runs along the lengthwise grain of the material. Cut a piece of lining and a piece of *lightweight* interlining (for information on the types of interlining see pages 19 and 20) exactly the same size as the swags material.

3 If you are making an inset frill, machine stitch the finished frill to the lower edge of the swag material right sides and raw edges together, placing the frill so that it is 1.5cm (½in) from each raw side edge of the swag material. A handmade set-on frill or ready-made fringing should, of course, be stitched on after the swags have been completed, but before they are gathered. Do not press the frill down, but leave it as machine stitched, pointing towards the inside of the swag material.

4 Lay the interlining on the table, and place the swag material on top of it so that the right side of the material is facing upwards. Pin the two layers together down the centre from top to bottom.

5 Lay the lining on top of the swag material, right sides together, and pin through all layers along 3 sides, leaving the top of the swags open. Then machine stitch along these 3 sides 1.5cm (½in) from the edge, again leaving the top open. Remove the pins along this seam, but not those holding the swag material to the interlining down the centre. Press along the seam to embed the stitches. Trim the interlining close to the machine stitches and turn the swags right side out. Press the edge flat along the seam.

6 Turn 1.5cm (½in) of lining to the wrong side and press a sharp fold in this turning; then open up the turning again. Machine stitch 2cm (¾in)-wide soft Velcro to the top of the lining *only*, placing the top edge of the Velcro along the pressed fold line. The Velcro should end and begin as close to the side seams as possible (see diagram of the back of the finished swags below). Now trim 1.5cm (½in) off the edge of the interlining along the top. Fold 1.5cm (½in) of the swag material over the interlining to the wrong side, then again turn under the lining along the pressed fold line. Hand stitch the top of the swags together. Press the seam.

7 Once the swag has been seamed, the 2cm (¾in)-wide gathering tape (see page 50) can be stitched in place. The tape should run from the top of the swag to the bottom, beginning just below the Velcro. The sample swags and tails will be fixed to a pelmet board which is wide enough for only 2 swags, so in this case there would be 3 strips of gathering tape (see positions in diagram below). Both ends of each strip of tape should be folded under and the gathering cords pulled clear. First machine stitch a strip of tape to each side edge of the swag, stitching through all the layers and

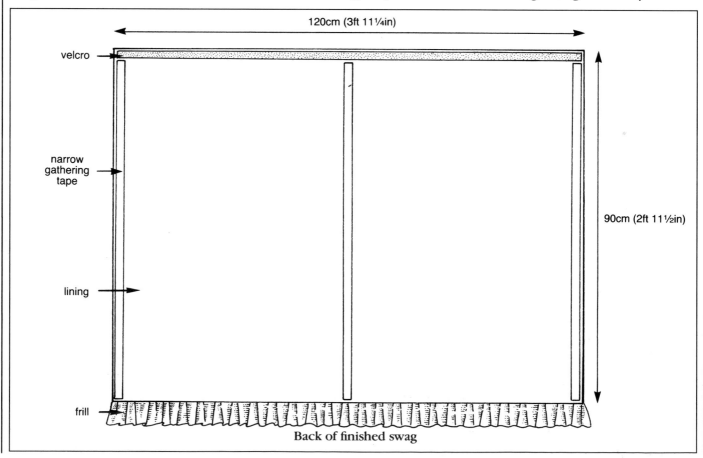

Back of finished swag

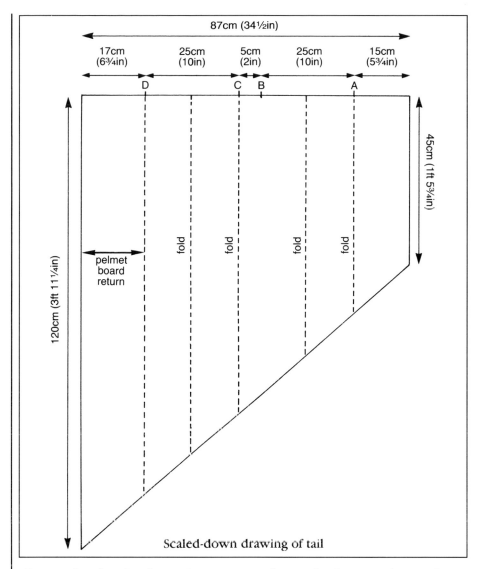

Scaled-down drawing of tail

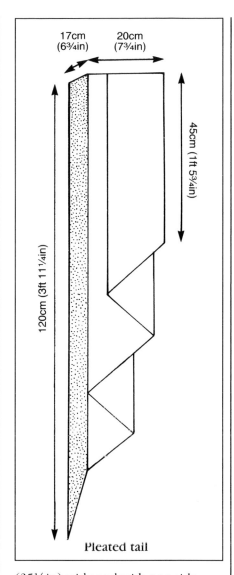

Pleated tail

all around each strip of tape close to the edge. Then remove the pins down the centre of the swag and stitch a strip of gathering tape down the centre in the same way.

8 Knot the cords at the bottom of each gathering tape. Then pull the cords from the top to gather the swag vertically, thus forming two swags; knot the cords together at the top of the swags.

Making the tails

1 Make a scaled-down drawing of the tails on graph paper and cut it out. The dimensions of the sample tail are shown above. For any other window the finished flat width of the tail can be the same as for the sample tail, but the long drop at the side edge should be at least half the total drop of the curtains. The inside

edge can be the same drop as the swags. Mark the positions of A, B, C and D on the paper tail as shown on the diagram above.

2 Fold the paper to test the shape of the pleats. Fold A to B and then fold C to D. Also fold back the side edge the depth of the pelmet return (see diagram above right). If you like the proportions of the pleats and the look of the tail, use the dimensions written on your paper template for the tail itself.

3 Make the desired handmade frill (see page 20) or purchase a ready-made trimming such as fringing. You will need enough trimming to cover the diagonal edge of each tail.

4 For the sample tail you would first cut a piece of material 90cm

(35½in) wide and with one side edge 1.23m (4ft ¼in) long and the other 48cm (1ft 6¾in) long. This allows for 1.5cm (½in) seams. Be sure to cut the material so that the drop runs along the lengthwise grain of the material. Cut a piece of lining and a piece of lightweight interlining exactly the same size. The wrong side of the tail will show at two places along the lower edge, so the last 30cm (12in) of the lining at the lower edge should be the main tail material (or a contrasting colour if desired).

5 If you are using a handmade inset frill, machine stitch the finished frill to the diagonal edge of the tail material with right sides and raw edges together, placing the frill so that it is 1.5cm (½in) from each raw side edge of the tail material. A

97

Because two such strong contrasting colours have been used in these swags and tails (previous pages) this elegant window treatment becomes the focal point of the drawing room.

handmade set-on frill or ready-made fringing should, of course, be stitched on once the tail has been completed, but before pleating. Do not press the frill down, but leave it as stitched pointing towards the inside of the material.

6 Lay the interlining on the table, and place the tail material on top of it so that the right side of the material is facing upwards. Lay the lining on top of the tail material, with right sides together and pin all the layers together around 3 edges, leaving the longer side edge open. Then machine stitch along the pinned sides 1.5cm (½in) from the edge. Remove the pins. Press along the seam to embed the stitches. Trim the interlining close to the machine stitches and turn the tail right side out. Press the edges along the seam.

7 Machine stitch a 17cm (6¾in)-long piece of 2cm (¾-in)-wide soft Velcro to the lining along the seam at the top of the tail. The Velcro should be placed on the right side of the lining right along the seamline and should begin 1.5cm (½in) from the raw edge at the long side edge of the tail. The tail will hang along the return of the pelmet board from this piece of Velcro. Now trim 1.5cm (½in) off the side edge of the interlining. Turn 1.5cm (½in) of the tail material over the interlining to the wrong side all along the open edge of the tail. Turn under the same amount along the open edge of the lining and hand stitch the final edge of the tail together. Press the seam. Make the second tail in the same way, but reversing the shaping.

Pleating the tail
1 Mark points A, B, C and D on the top of the tail, following the scale drawing made in steps 1 and 2. Then fold the pleats, folding A to B and C to D. To fix the pleats in place, oversew (U.S. 'overcast') the tops of the pleats with a strong needle and strong matching thread.

2 Hand sew a plain heading tape 2cm (¾in) wide along the top edge of the tail from the shorter, inner edge to the beginning of the Velcro. The tape should be sewn *only* to the top edge of the tail. It must swing free from the tail so that it can be stapled to the *top* side of the pelmet board.

Hanging the swags and tails
As for most pelmets, the pelmet board for swags and tails must have stiff Velcro attached to the edge of the board from wall to wall. When hanging the swags and tails, begin by sticking the Velcro on the swags in place along the front of the pelmet board. Do not worry about the fact that the two lower corners of the swags have nothing to fix onto. This does not matter at all. They hang beautifully on their own, and the tails will cover the edges.

Make sure that the swags have been gathered just the right amount to hang to the required depth. If necessary, you can readjust the gathers while they are hanging by merely undoing the knots at the bottom of the gathering tape.

Once the swags are in place you can hang the tails. Attach the Velcro at the side edges to the returns, and then staple the heading tape (along the top of the rest of the tail) to the top of the pelmet board. Keep the top of the tail level with the top of the swags.

Chapter Eight

AUSTRIAN AND ROMAN BLINDS

There are many situations in which you may not be able to use ordinary curtains
for a window treatment, either because they would not be suitable or because there
would not be room for them. In these cases, the obvious alternative is to use blinds.
This chapter covers the making of Austrian and Roman blinds. I often use one or
the other of these when designing window treatments for kitchens or bathrooms.
They are both economical in terms of curtain material and very practical for
restricted spaces, as well as being stunning designs in their own right.

AUSTRIAN BLINDS

Austrian blinds are gathered horizontally across the heading, and as they are pulled up, they are also gathered vertically, at intervals across the blind. You would be wrong to dismiss this window treatment as rather passé. It is not, and should not be regarded as such. The reason the Austrian blind now has a 'bad press' is that it suffered great indignities during the 1970s and '80s, when yuppies tended to use the design far too frequently on unsuitable windows, covering them in pink bows whenever possible! But if designed and used with sensitivity they can be very elegant.

History of Austrian blinds

The special heyday for the Austrian blind was at the end of the seventeenth century. It was then known as a 'pull-up'. But it served a different purpose than it does today. In the seventeenth century no one was really thinking of curtaining windows with a view to keeping out the cold, let alone creating a decorative interior design. Instead, pull-ups were conceived out of a necessity to filter strong sunlight. People had become aware of the terrible damage that sunlight could inflict on pictures and furniture by making them fade.

There were two main reasons why pull-ups were preferred to long curtains in those days. Firstly, they were safer; draughts could blow long curtains onto naked candle flames. Secondly, pull-ups did not obscure the beautifully carved architraves on either side of the window.

Suitable places for Austrian blinds

Austrian blinds are wonderful in kitchens, where cabinets so often go right up to the window sills. They have the added advantage of requiring no interlining which would retain dirt, steam and kitchen smells.

In terms of design, Austrian blinds are suitable for kitchens because their graceful swags give a break from the endless sharp squares and rectangles formed by kitchen units, ovens, refrigerators and tiles. They are also sensible because they pull up high above the window sills, leaving no material flapping in the way, disturbing plants and china on the sill.

Austrian blinds are equally suitable for bathrooms, and for the same reasons. They so effectively dissolve that clinical atmosphere.

In children's bedrooms you may wish to keep the space below the window free for toy boxes or shelves, so again Austrian blinds would be the answer, especially for girls' rooms.

Long curtains can be very awkward on windows in stairwells, since the lower edge of the curtain would have to be cut at a diagonal to accommodate the steps. This can look a little strange, so beautifully dressed and elaborate Austrian blinds would be a better option in this instance as well.

Finished drop of Austrian blinds

Instead of using a pelmet board to hang the blind from, you will need a timber batten 5cm by 2.5cm (2in by 1in). The batten can be fixed to the wall just above the window architrave, with a 5cm (2in) side flush with the wall. Alternatively the batten can be fixed to the top of the architrave itself, level with its top.

The blind is hung from the batten by means of Velcro, so to determine the finished drop required for your Austrian blind you must measure from the top of the batten position to just below the sill.

Keep in mind that these blinds take up one third of the window space when pulled up and will therefore obscure some of the light coming in the window. If you wish, you can overcome this drawback by fixing the batten well above the architrave to create extra height.

Complete instructions for preparing the batten and fixing it in place are given on page 106.

Finished flat drop of blind

When completely closed, the blind must never have a straight lower edge, but must have definite curves created by the swags of the blind. This means that the blind is gathered vertically at the lower edge even when closed, and the finished flat length of the blind is longer than the finished drop of the gathered, hanging blind. The amount of extra material needed to ensure this effect is about 30cm (12in).

Width of the blind before pleating

You can use pencil pleating for the heading of the blind, but it requires a finished flat blind width at least 2½ times the width of the window. The pencil pleats would not be full enough without this amount of fullness. Unfortunately this fullness makes the blind rather billowy, and the whole window treatment, instead of being subtle, becomes overpowering.

The blind looks much better when it is only about twice the width of the window before pleating. As a result I prefer to use a French-pleated heading which is much better suited to this width.

Width of the blind after pleating

The width of the blind after pleating is, of course, determined by the width of the batten. The batten should extend past the architrave by 2cm (¾in) on each side. The finished pleated blind should then extend a little past the ends of the batten so that the batten is obscured sufficiently from view. If your blind has, however, a frill along three sides, the finished blind itself should be pleated to the exact width of the batten. The frill will then extend past the batten on either side to hide it.

Handmade frills

If the blind is to be set in a recess, only the lower edge should have a frill. Any vertical frills on a blind set in a recess would be likely to rub against the adjacent walls when being opened and closed and would look too cramped in the narrow space. However, in other situations a blind looks wonderful with a frill along three sides (see page 20 for *Handmade frills*).

If you are making a frill, calculate the material quantity accordingly.

If the cords for vertically gathering, or pulling up, the Austrian blind are set well in from the edges, pretty 'tails' like these (see right) are formed at each side.

Never skimp on calculations – there is nothing more annoying than not having quite enough material.

The sample blind
The blind used as the example in the instructions has a French-pleated heading and a frill around the remaining three sides.

The finished drop of the sample blind and the batten width are as follows:

– Finished blind drop 1.80m (5ft 11in)
– Batten width 1.30m (4ft 3¼in)

To calculate the cutting length, add the hem allowance, the turn-down allowance at the top for French pleats (see page 57) and the excess for swags to the finished drop:

Finished drop	180cm	(5ft 11in)
Turn-down	18cm	(7in)
Hem allowance	1.5cm	(½in)
Swags excess	30cm	(12in)
Cutting length	229.5cm	(7ft 6½in)

The finished flat drop is calculated by adding the finished drop and the length of the swags excess, which in this case adds up to a total of 210cm (6ft 11in).

For this particular window treatment you should use 2 widths of curtain material. It does not matter whether the width of the material from selvedge to selvedge is 120cm (47in) or 137cm (54in); 2 widths will be adequate since together they are roughly twice the width of the batten.

When buying material, remember to add the length of the pattern repeat to each of the widths to be cut, so that you have an allowance for pattern-matching (see page 37).

The number of swags chosen for the sample blind is 3, which is highly recommended for this particular width. Too many swags will make the design look too fussy and it will lose much of its elegance.

Austrian blinds, like Roman blinds, can often be used in conjunction with curtains and pelmets (as seen left), but they must be carefully planned to fit into the overall design.

Lining and interlining
Austrian blinds are not interlined, as they must be essentially light and bouncy. For pencil-pleat, French-pleat and goblet-pleat headings, however, you will need a strip of medium-weight interlining to insert from edge to edge of the top of the blind, along the heading. When using fusible buckram in a heading it is essential to place interlining between the buckram and the main material. But with pencil-pleat tape the interlining is used merely to enhance the look of the heading by giving it far more body and depth.

The interlining should be the same depth as the chosen type of heading. The sample blind has a French-pleated heading, so it requires interlining the same depth as the fusible buckram – or in this case 15cm (6in).

The amount of lining required for an Austrian blind is the same as the amount of main material.

Table clamps
Use your table clamps just as you would when making curtains. Whenever you are pinning the long seams, the clamps will help to hold the layers of fabric together. Also, they are essential when positioning one large piece of fabric on top of another, as they will keep the fabric on the table from slipping while the top layer is being smoothed in place on top of it.

Making the blind
1 Cut the widths for the blind. The widths must be joined in the same way as for pelmets – that is with no seam running up the centre. So if you are using only 2 widths of material you will have to cut one of the widths in half lengthwise and sew a half width to either side of the whole width. Pattern-join the widths (see page 44). Cut and join the lining in the same way. Press all seams to embed the machine stitches, then press the seams open.

2 Make an inset frill long enough to go along the two sides and the lower edge of the blind (see page 20 through page 26 for instructions on how to make a selection of *Handmade frills*).

3 Placing the beginning and the end of the frill 18cm (7in) from the top edge, pin the frill to the main material around 3 sides, with right sides and raw edges together. This allows for the 18cm (7in) heading allowance at the top of the blind. Machine stitch the frill to the blind material 1.5cm (½in) from the raw edge, removing the pins as you stitch. Then lay the material wrong side down on the table. Keeping the frill lying towards the centre of the material, use a few pins to secure the corners in place flat against the blind. This is done as a safeguard to ensure that the frill does not catch at the corners when the lining is machine stitched over it.

4 With the blind material still facing upwards on the table, lay the lining on top of it, right sides and raw edges together. Pin the lining in place around the previously stitched sides. Turn the blind over so that the main material is facing upwards, and machine stitch the lining to the blind material, working the stitches just inside the first row and again beginning and ending 18cm (7in) from the top. This stitching is worked inside the first line in order to conceal the first line when the blind is turned right side out. Press to embed the stitches. Trim the seam allowance to about 5mm (¼in). Turn the blind right side out and press the seam flat.

5 Clamp the lower edge of the blind wrong side up onto one long edge of the table. Holding the top of the blind stretched from the clamps, pull firmly on both fabric layers to take out the slack. Insert a few pins around the blind so that the layers will remain together.

Making the heading
1 Keeping the blind wrong side up, turn it so that it is lying lengthwise on the table. Remembering that the finished flat drop includes the swags excess, measure the finished flat drop up from the bottom of the blind. Measure, mark and join the marks along the top of the blind as described in step 1 on page 49. Then cut *the lining only* along the line just drawn.

2 Insert a 15cm (6in)-wide strip of medium-weight interlining along the heading from edge to edge between the lining and the main material, with the top edge level with the raw edge of the lining.

3 Insert the buckram and complete the heading following steps 3–6 on page 59.

The vertical gathers

Before the heading pleats are worked the plastic rings should be sewn onto the back of the blind. The finished blind is gathered vertically (at the back) with cords, which are held in place by these plastic rings. You should use rings no more than 1.5cm (½in) in diameter.

Sewing on plastic rings

1 When sewing the rings to the back of the blind, use a thread that matches the blind material, and stitch right through both the lining and the blind material. Do not worry that the stitches will show on the front; they are well hidden due to the design of the blind. Beginning at the lower edge, sew rings to the wrong side of the blind along one side edge, spacing them about 15cm (6in) apart and placing the last ring 25cm (10in) from the top of the blind (the rings have to stop clear of the heading so as not to interfere with it). The sample blind would therefore have about 14 rings along the side edge. Only the rings on the lower edge will receive much pressure. The other plastic rings are there purely to guide the cords, so you need not sew them on as conscientiously as you sew on the ones on the lower edge.

2 Sew rings along the other side edge in corresponding positions.

3 With the blind clamped to the table wrong side up, divide the lower edge into 3 sections in order to mark the positions of 2 more vertical rows of rings. Using the long folding ruler as a guide to ensure straight lines, sew on 2 more vertical rows of rings in positions corresponding to the rings at the side edges. When the blind is eventually pulled up on cords

Back of Austrian blind

threaded through these 4 lines of rings, 3 swags will form.

Making the pleats

Calculate for the heading pleats as instructed on page 58. Then make the pleats following steps 1–7 on page 59.

After the heading has been pleated sew 2cm (¾in)-wide soft Velcro to the top of the heading as given for a pencil-pleated pelmet in step 8 on page 73.

Hanging the blind

1 Before the batten is fixed to the wall it must be properly prepared. The batten is eventually fixed in place so that one of the 5cm (2in) sides is flush with the wall. (See page 102 for the width of the batten across top of window.) To prepare the batten, first cover it with a piece of the main material, using a staple gun. This is a professional touch which will ensure that if the batten is ever visible it will not be conspicuous. Then staple a strip of stiff 2cm (¾in)-wide Velcro across the 5cm (2in)-deep front of the batten (along the top edge).

2 Screw eyes are fixed to the underside 2.5cm (1in)-edge of the batten to receive the cords. With a bradawl, make holes at each end of the batten to correspond to the rings at the side edges of the blind. Screw a 4cm (1½in)-long screw eye into each of these holes. Divide the space between these 2 eyes by 3, and insert 2 more screw eyes in the same way. The positions of these 2 screw eyes will correspond to the positions of the other 2 rows of rings on the blind.

3 Drill a hole at each end of the batten from front to back. The batten is now ready to be fixed to the wall with a screw placed through each of these holes. You would be well advised to have a professional fix the batten in place to ensure that it is securely attached.

4 Once the batten is securely in place, hang the blind from the Velcro. You must now feed cord through the rings. Cut 4 pieces of strong nylon blind cord about 4m (4½yd) long (they will be trimmed later). Beginning at the first ring at the lower edge of the right side of the blind at the back, feed the cord through all the rings up the side edge and across the underside of the batten through all 4 screw eyes. Repeat this up the remaining rows of rings, always feeding the cord from right to left through the screw eyes on the batten, so that only the screw on the far left has all 4 cords passing through it (see the diagram on the facing page).

5 In order to ensure that the blind does not sag into the window recess and that the lower edge – even though swagged – will remain parallel to the window sill, you must attach a length of dowelling to the rings along the lower edge of the blind. You will need a wooden dowelling rod 1.5cm (½in) in diameter and the same length as the batten, which means, in the case of the sample blind, 1.30m (4ft 3¼in).

Cut a strip of lining 10cm by 133cm (4in by 4ft 4¼in). Turn under 1.5cm (½in) at both short ends and press. Then turn under 1.5cm (½in) along both long sides and press. Place wrong sides and folded edges together, and machine stitch close to the fold and across one short end. Sew 4 plastic rings to the seamed edge of the tube, one at each end and the other 2 evenly spaced between. Slide the rod into the fabric tube, then hand sew the opening together. Now tie the rings along the lower edge of the blind to the rings on the covered rod. Do not trim the ends of the cord, but tie them up instead, so that you can later untie these knots to remove the blind for cleaning. Never hang an Austrian blind without a rod tied in place.

6 Pull the strings to adjust them, so that the rod at the lower edge of the blind is level and the blind is fully down. Remember that when it is down, the lower edge must still be swagged and the drop of the blind should come to just below the sill. With the blind closed in this position, cut the 4 cords so that about 15cm (6in) of each cord remains below the last screw eye. Knot these ends to one end of a 5cm (2in) S-hook. Sew through the knot to ensure that it will not come undone. Attach a decorative bell-pull rope with a tassel to the other end of the S-hook. When the blind is pulled up, the rope is wrapped around a brass cleat attached to the architrave.

Cleaning the blind
When the Austrian blind needs cleaning, simply untie the cords at the lower edge and remove the blind. Leave the cord in place for the blind's return.

ROMAN BLINDS
A Roman blind can be a wonderful window treatment, given the right situation. It has the advantage of being even more economical in terms of material than an Austrian blind because, when closed, the flat Roman blind covers only the window area. Suitable places for Roman blinds are basically the same

as those for Austrian blinds. You can make your choice depending on which design you prefer, with the exception of bay windows, where Roman blinds are more suitable.

There is another instance in which an Austrian blind cannot be substituted for a Roman blind, and that is in situations where a Roman blind is used as a decorative addition to a window treatment with curtains and a pelmet. In these cases the blind is not added primarily for its function, but more to give a 'third dimension' to the overall design.

Roman blinds in bay windows
One particularly dramatic and decorative window treatment using Roman blinds is well worth a special mention. The setting is a bay window with a window seat. You can create a truly theatrical look by hanging huge dress curtains at each side of the bay with a beautiful pelmet along the top of the windows. The dress curtains, although not functional, should look full, so the correct number of widths must be used in each of them. They should be a little longer than floor length and held back with low tiebacks. To complete the 'stage' effect, a Roman blind is then added to cover each of the three windows, stopping just at the sill above the window seat.

Suitable materials for Roman blinds
Unlike Austrian blinds, which should be light in appearance, Roman blinds look especially good in some of the heavier materials. Linens and corded silks are my favourite materials for Roman blinds. Because plain colours are usually used for Roman blinds, the textures of these two types of materials will provide a lovely feature.

Finished drop of Roman blinds
Like an Austrian blind, the Roman blind is hung by Velcro from a batten 5cm by 2.5cm (2in by 1in). The batten is fixed either just above the window architrave or to the top of the architrave itself.

Unlike an Austrian blind, this blind should not be hung much higher than the top of the window.

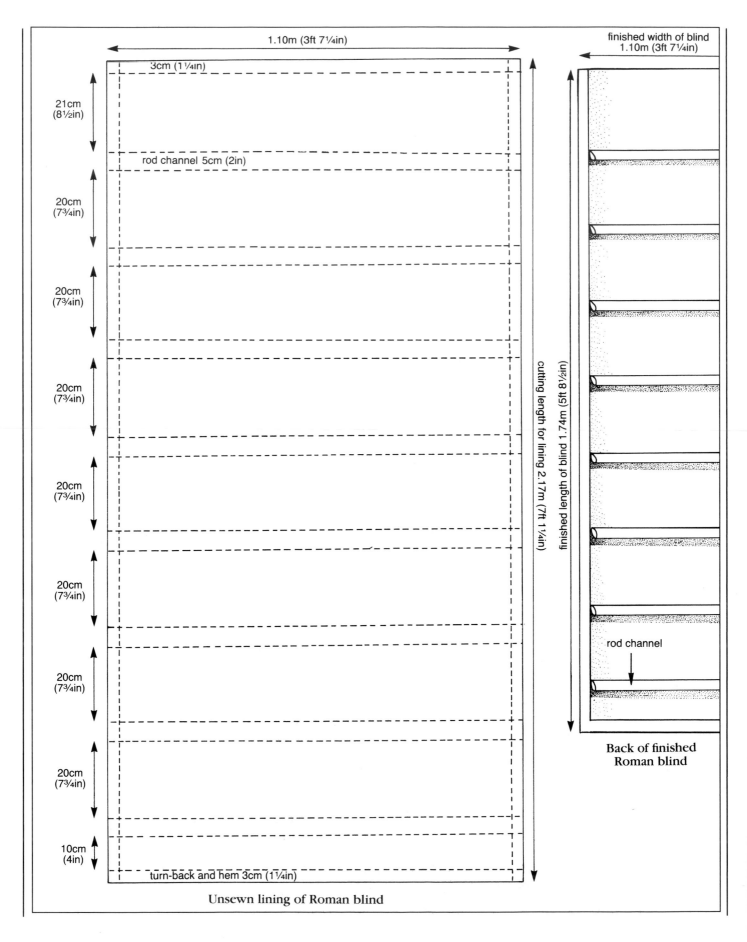

1.10m (3ft 7¼in)

3cm (1¼in)

21cm (8½in)

rod channel 5cm (2in)

20cm (7¾in)

20cm (7¾in)

20cm (7¾in)

20cm (7¾in)

20cm (7¾in)

20cm (7¾in)

20cm (7¾in)

10cm (4in)

turn-back and hem 3cm (1¼in)

cutting length for lining 2.17m (7ft 1¼in)

finished length of blind 1.74m (5ft 8½in)

Unsewn lining of Roman blind

finished width of blind
1.10m (3ft 7¼in)

rod channel

**Back of finished
Roman blind**

It does not have the fullness that the Austrian blind has, and therefore could not create the optical illusion of heightening the window treatment in the same way.

To determine the finished drop of the Roman blind, you must measure from the *top* of the batten to just below the sill. The batten is prepared and fixed in place in much the same way as the batten for the Austrian blind.

Finished width of the blind

The batten should extend past the window architrave by 2cm (¾in) on each side. The blind is not gathered across the heading at all, so the finished width of the blind is the same width as the batten.

Fan trimming

Fan trimming cannot, of course, be used along the sides because the blind forms horizontal folds as it is pulled. The lower edge, however, can be trimmed, and what I find extremely pretty as a finish is a row of pleated fans. The fans are very ornate and so manage to soften the hard lines of the blind itself. They are very easy to make and will give your blind immense visual impact.

Always include the depth of the fans when calculating the finished drop. Instructions for making the pleated fans follow the blind-making instructions (see pages 111 and 112).

The sample blind

The finished drop and the batten width of the sample blind in the following instructions are:

– Finished blind drop 1.74m (5ft 8½in)
– Batten width 1.10m (3ft 7¼in)

To calculate the cutting length for the blind material, simply add on a 5cm (2in) turn-down allowance at the top and a 5cm (2in) hem allowance. This would make the cutting length for the sample blind 1.84m (6ft ½in).

The finished width of the blind is the same as the width of the batten. Again, to determine the cutting width, simply add on a 5cm (2in) turn-back at each side. This means a 1.20m (3ft 11¼in) cutting width for the sample blind.

If you should have to use more than one width of material for a Roman blind, you must not have a central seam. The excess must be added at either side of the central width, and if you are using a print, the pieces must be pattern-matched.

Lining and interlining

Roman blinds are not interlined. The amount of lining required will be more than the amount of main material. This is because channels are formed in the lining to hold the wooden rods.

The cutting width of the lining is the exact width of the finished blind. This is because the side edges, when turned under, do not extend to the very edge of the finished blind but 3cm (1¼in) inside it.

The cutting length is determined by adding to the finished drop: 3cm (1¼in) for a turn-down at the top and an extra 5cm (2in) allowance for each rod channel. These channels take the form of narrow flaps across the lining.

The diagram on the facing page shows the positions of the channels on the sample-blind lining. Eight channels are used in this instance. The space between each rod is 20cm (7¾in), and this means that when the blind is pulled up – and the rods are thereby pulled together – a fold, or 'pleat', about 10cm (4in) deep will form between each pair of rods. I recommend this depth for most Roman blinds, so you should always space the rods about 20cm (8in) apart, whatever the drop of the finished blind.

The wooden rods

The wooden rods inserted in the channels should be no more than 1.5cm (½in) in diameter. Each dowelling rod should be as long as the finished width of the lining. Because the lining, when folded back, is 6cm (2½in) narrower than the finished blind, each rod for the sample blind should be 1.04m (3ft 4¾in) long.

Besides the rods for the channels, you will need a flat 5mm by 3cm (¼in by 1in) batten to give a little extra weight to the bottom of the blind. It should be the same length as the width of the finished blind, since it is inserted in the hem of the blind material.

Making the blind

1 Cut the blind material 1.20m by 1.84m (3ft 11¼in by 6ft ½in). This allows for a 5cm (2in) turn-back allowance around all edges. Forming diagonals at the corners, turn 5cm (2in) to the wrong side along all the four edges of the material; press.

2 Cut the lining 1.10m by 2.17m (3ft 7¼in by 7ft 1¼in) to allow for a 3cm (1¼in) turn-back all around the edge and 5cm (2in) extra for each of the 8 rod channels. Turn 3cm (1¼in) to the wrong side along all 4 edges of the lining and press.

3 Mark the positions of the rod channels 20cm (7¾in) apart (see the lining diagram for positions). Fold the fabric in half between each pair of marked lines, placing wrong sides together, and machine stitch to form the channels. Make sure during this process to leave the side edges turned under.

4 Cut a piece of soft 2cm (¾in)-wide Velcro the same measurement as the batten from which the blind will be hung. Leaving 3cm (1¼in) of Velcro extending past each side edge of the lining, machine stitch the Velcro to the top of the lining, with the top edge of the Velcro along the fold line of the turn-down and working the stitches close to the 4 edges of the Velcro. The ends of the Velcro will be hand stitched to the blind material after the lining has been sewn in place.

5 Clamp one side edge of the blind material right side down to one long edge of the table. With the wrong sides together, pin the lining to the blind material so that the top edges are aligned and so that the side edges and lower edge of the lining are 3cm (1¼in) from the edges of the blind material. Clamping and re-clamping as necessary, pin the lining in place around all 4 sides; place pins along each channel across the width of the blind to keep them

firmly in position. Then slipstitch the lining to the blind around 3 sides; leaving the ends of the channels and the lower edge of the lining open. Now slip the flat batten into the hem of the blind material, then slipstitch along the lower edge of the lining hem. Remove all pins except the pins along each channel. Hand sew the ends of the Velcro to the heading.

6 Using matching thread and with the wrong side facing upwards, machine stitch the lining to the blind material along each channel seam. It is essential that the lining be firmly secured to the front of the blind. The only instance where I would consider hand stitching the channels in place is on a fine plain silk. For materials with more texture, such as linen or corded silk,

Roman blinds are an excellent choice when total simplicity is required in a window treatment. This thinly striped blind (above) is a good example of this spare elegance.

Because Roman blinds take up so little space they can be used with a fixed heading, as seen here (facing page) where well-formed pencil pleats are the focus of the curtain design.

or materials with a print, the machine stitching on the front of the blind will not be at all noticeable. But do match your machine thread carefully.

7 Slip the rods into the channels, and hand stitch the ends to close them. Sew two 1.5cm (½in) plastic rings to each channel, placing each one about 12cm (4½in) from end of channel. You will need a ring at the centre of each rod only if the blind is over 1.35cm (4½ft) wide.

Hanging the blind

1 To prepare the batten, follow step 1 for hanging the Austrian blind.

2 Position screw eyes on the underside of the batten as in step 2 for the Austrian blinds, but using only 3 screw eyes: one at each end of the batten, 12cm (4½in) from the edge (above the plastic rings at the ends of the rods) and a third at the far right at the very edge of the batten through which both strings can be channelled.

3 Follow step 3 as for the Austrian blind.

4 Once the batten is securely in place, hang the blind from the Velcro. Cut 2 pieces of strong nylon blind cord 4m (4½yd) long (they will be trimmed later). Tie one end of the first length of cord to the ring on the left side of the lowest channel. Feed the cord through the rings along this side of the blind, then through all 3 screw eyes on the underside of the batten. Tie the other length of cord to the other ring on the lowest channel, and feed the cord through the rings on that side of the blind, but threading it through only the 2 screw eyes on the right side of the batten.

5 Pull the cords to adjust them. With the blind down and fully extended, trim the 2 cords so that about 15cm (6in) of each cord remains below the last screw eye. Knot these ends to one end of a 5cm (2in) S-hook. Sew through the knot to ensure that it will not come undone. Attach a decorative bell-pull rope with a tassel to the other end of the

S-hook. When the blind is pulled up, the rope is wrapped around a brass cleat attached to the architrave. For cleaning, the blind can be removed as for the Austrian blind.

Dimensions for fans

Fans along the lower edge of the Roman blind look especially effective when made in a contrasting colour. Although the width of the blind will obviously influence the size of each fan, the fans look best when they are anywhere between 12cm and 25cm (4¾in and 9¾in) wide. An uneven number of fans across the blind looks much better than an even number, so the sample blind could have 5 fans, each 22cm (8⅝in) wide (see the dimensions on

the illustration below).

Each fan is made from a simple seamed fabric rectangle which is pleated accordion-fashion and then secured at the centre so that when the pleats on either side drop down they form a semicircle. The finished flat length of the fan before pleating is calculated by adding about 22 per cent onto the measurement of the finished width. For the sample fan that would make the length 27cm (10½in).

Making the fans

1 Always test the dimensions of the flat width of the fan before cutting the material. Cut a piece of paper 27cm by 22cm (10½in by 8⅝in). Fold down 1.5cm (½in) at the top of

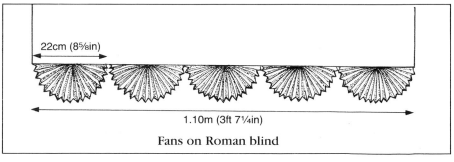

22cm (8⅝in)

1.10m (3ft 7¼in)

Fans on Roman blind

the piece of paper across the 22cm (8⅝in) width. Then 1.5cm (½in) below this fold line, fold again but in the other direction. Continue in this way, folding a pleat every 1.5cm (½in), first in one direction and then in the opposite direction until the entire length of the rectangle of paper has been pleated. Pinch the pleats together at the centre, and let the two sides fan downwards, meeting at the centre to form a semicircle. If the size is right, then you can proceed to use these dimensions for the fan. Add length if necessary.

2 Now cut a piece of material 25cm by 57cm (9⅝in by 22in) for one fan.

3 Fold the piece of material in half widthwise, right sides together. Using a matching thread, machine stitch the two long side edges 1.5cm (½in) from the raw edge, leaving the bottom edge open. Press to embed the stitches, trim the corners and turn right side out. Press along the seams.

4 Turn 1.5cm (½in) to the inside along both raw edges on the open end and press. Machine stitch this side together close to the edge. Press the seam.

5 Fold down 1.5cm (½in) at the top of the seamed rectangle along the

edge just seamed; press. Then, 1.5cm (½in) below this fold line, fold again, but in the other

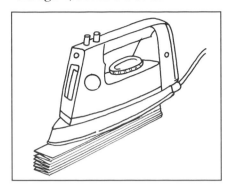

direction, and press. Continue forming accordion pleats until the entire piece has been pleated.

6 Pinch the pleats together at the centre, and hand sew the stack of folds together at one side of the 1.5cm (½in)-wide pleats, but leaving the first 1.5cm (½in) at the top of the fan unstitched so that it can be opened out. This edge will be sewn to the back of the blind. Now hand sew the two edges at the centre of the semicircle together, from the centre to outer edge (see below).

7 Make 4 more fans in the same way. Placing the top 1.5cm (½in) of each fan on the wrong side of the blind and letting the fan hang from it, hand sew it to the lower edge of the blind.

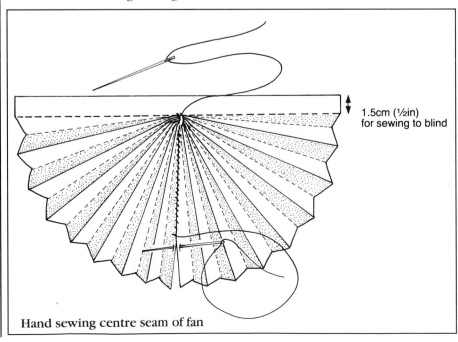

1.5cm (½in) for sewing to blind

Hand sewing centre seam of fan

Chapter Nine

TIE-BACKS,
ROSETTES AND BOWS

Although decorative finishes such as tie-backs, rosettes and bows are the last things you make for your window treatment, you should never treat them as an afterthought. They are an integral part of your curtain design and should be planned from the very first stages, as part of your 7-Prong Plan. These details may be small, but they play a vital role in the overall impact of your window treatment.

TIE-BACKS

A tie-back must earn its place in a window treatment and serve a definite purpose. It must not merely be made and hooked in place purely because you have some remnants to use up, or because you have just learned how to make one and are dying to try out your skills!

Reasons for tie-backs

The tie-back has one predominant function and that is to draw the curtains off the window to admit maximum light. This is, of course, a necessity for curtains with a fixed heading, such as static pole-headed curtains and Velcro-headed curtains both with stand-ups (see pages 62 and 64).

You should also, however, note the visual effect of tie-backs; they give the curtains an especially graceful shape. This shape, which tempts the eye upwards, greatly enhances the elegant length and hang of the curtains.

Choosing your tie-back

Make an effort to choose the right type of tie-back for your particular window treatment, paying careful attention to details in the pelmet or curtain. For instance, caterpillar tie-backs are perfect for curtains that are slotted onto a pole through a casing because they echo the ruched heading.

If you prefer, you can use purchased tie-backs. Ropes with tassels make a lovely addition to some window treatments. And brass tie-backs can be extremely attractive and, in some cases, far more suitable for a particular treatment than tie-backs made of material.

Size of finished tie-backs

I never make a material tie-back before the curtains are hanging. No two window treatments are absolutely identical. So once you have hung the curtains, get someone else to hold a soft tape measure around the curtain. You can then stand at a distance and decide on the length, width and exact position of the tie-back. After making these decisions, you are ready to screw the brass receiver hook in place and make the tie-backs.

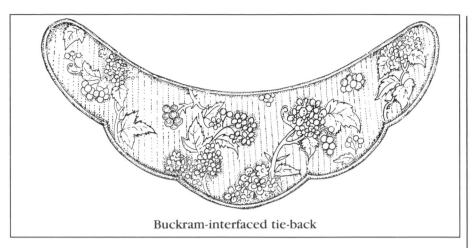

Buckram-interfaced tie-back

BUCKRAM-INTERFACED TIE-BACKS

Buckram-interfaced tie-backs are flat. The buckram used is thicker and stiffer than the fusible buckram used in hand-pleated headings. This type of tie-back is crescent-shaped, so that it fits gracefully around the curtain. The edges of the crescent shape are either plain or scalloped in various ways and are piped (U.S. 'corded') in a contrasting colour to accentuate the curves.

Materials required

When making a buckram-interfaced tie-back you will need the following:

– Main material for both sides of each tie-back
– Contrasting material for the piping
– Piping cord
– Heavyweight buckram
– Medium-weight interlining
– 4 rings 1.5cm (½in) in diameter
– Matching thread

The amounts of material required depend, of course, on the size of the tie-backs. You will usually have enough remnants after making your pelmet and curtains to make the tie-backs. However, if you do not, then carefully calculate the amounts needed after making your template.

Making buckram tie-back

1 After measuring around your curtain to decide on the width needed, make a paper template of the desired finished shape. The tie-back used as the example (above) needs to be 64cm (25¼in) wide to accommodate the curtain. The lower

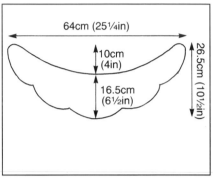

edge of the crescent shape is gently scalloped in a traditional manner.

2 With a pencil, draw around the template edge onto the buckram, then cut out the buckram along the pencil outline.

3 Cut 2 rectangular pieces of medium-weight interlining, each large enough to cover one side of the buckram shape. Place the piece of cut-out buckram on the ironing board and spray it with water. Place the interlining on top of it, and press with a hot iron. The combination of the heat, the water and the glue sizing in the buckram will cause the interlining to stick to the buckram. Trim off the excess interlining right up to the edge of the buckram so that it is *exactly* the same size as the buckram. Cover the other side of the buckram with medium-weight interlining in the same way you covered the first side.

Buckram-interfaced tie-backs can be made with curved edges (as above) or with smooth edges (as right), but they are always crescent shaped to fit around the curtains gracefully.

4 Draw around the shaped buckram piece onto the *right side* of the tie-back material. Cut out this fabric shape, cutting 1.5cm (½in) outside the line to allow for the seam. The pencil line is used as a guide for the position of the piping. Cut a second piece of tie-back material, the same size as the first, but omitting the pencil line.

5 Using contrasting material, cover enough piping cord to fit around the edge of the tie-back (see page 79 for covering piping cord). Placing right sides and raw edges together, machine stitch the piping to the main material along the pencil outline.

6 With the interlining facing the wrong side of the piped material, place the buckram on top of the material. Fold the seam allowance over the edge of the buckram and press all around the edge. Then place the wrong side of the second piece of tie-back material on top of the buckram. Fold the seam allowance on the material to the inside so that the fold line just meets the seam at the base of the piping and pin the material around the edge of the tie-back.

7 Before hand stitching this layer in place, attach the rings. Using a double thread, sew a 1.5cm (½in) ring to each end of the tie-back so

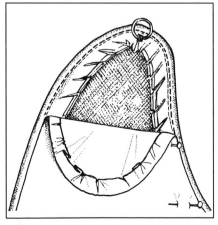

that it extends halfway past the piped edge. Then, using matching thread, slipstitch the remaining tie-back section in place. Make the second tie-back in exactly the same way as the first.

Plaited tie-back

PLAITED TIE-BACKS

Plaited tie-backs are highly fashionable. They look very attractive if you use a contrasting colour for one of the three sections of the plait. This fits in beautifully with a window treatment that uses the same contrasting colour in its pelmet as well.

The sample plaited tie-back
The tie-back used as the example in the instructions has a finished length of 60cm (23½in) and is 5cm (2in) wide after plaiting. Note that when you plait the stuffed tubes, you will lose 25 per cent of the original length. So be sure to add this amount to the desired finished length when deciding on the length of the strips for the tubes. It is probably best to add a little more than this just to be safe. You can then trim the tie-back before finishing off the end.

If you want a thinner or thicker plait than the sample one, just make the tubes narrower or wider as desired. What is essential is that the interlining stuffing should always be cut approximately 50 per cent wider than the tube material.

Materials for plaited tie-backs
For making plaited tie-backs the only materials required are as follows:

– Remnant of curtain material
– Medium-weight interlining
– Matching thread
– 4 rings 1.5cm (½in) in diameter

If you do not have enough curtain material left over, then determine the exact dimensions of the tube strips before purchasing any extra material.

Making plaited tie-backs
1 Cut 3 strips of material, each 9cm by 80cm (3½in by 2ft 7½in). (As suggested it is advisable to cut one of the strips in a contrasting colour.)

2 Fold one strip in half lengthwise, with right sides together. Machine stitch along the long side 1.5cm (½in) from the edge and across one short end. Do not press. Trim the seam to 8mm (¼in). Seam the remaining strips in the same way.

3 Using large scissors to push from the short seamed end, turn each tube right side out. Cut off the seam at the short end of each tube; its only purpose was to assist in turning the tubes right side out. Now it is removed so that the seam can be positioned up the centre of the back of the tube. *Never press the tie-back tubes* (except for tie-backs with 'ears').

4 Cut 3 strips of medium-weight interlining 13cm by 80cm (5in by 2ft 7½in).

5 Cut a piece of string 10cm (4in) longer than the tube, and tie it firmly to the neck of a slim teaspoon. Tie the other end of the string to one of the strips of interlining. Drop the spoon, handle first, down the tube. When the spoon appears at the other end of the tube, pull it to draw the interlining into the tube. The beginning of the interlining, where it is tied to the string, may need to be pinched together slightly before it will start to go down the tube, but once the end is in it will pull through smoothly. Pull the interlining through until the untied end of the interlining is level with the end of the tube. Now untie the string. Stuff the remaining tubes in exactly the same way.

6 Pull back 2cm (¾in) of material at one end of each tube, and trim 2cm (¾in) off the end of the interlining. It is necessary to remove this bulk so that the 3 tubes can now be sewn together at this end. Lay the tubes right side up, one on top of the other and with the seams at the

centre of the back, and machine stitch them together 1.5cm (½in) from the end.

7 Clamp the machine-stitched end to the edge of the table and plait the 3 tubes together; pin the ends together. Now check that the tie-back is the desired length, measuring from one raw edge to the other (the ends will not be folded back but bound with another piece of material). Unpin the ends and trim them if necessary. Then trim 2cm (¾in) off the end of the interlining inside each tube and machine stitch the ends together in the same way as at the beginning of the plait.

8 Now bind the ends of the tie-back. Using material that matches 2 of the tubes, cut a piece measuring 12cm by 7cm (4¾in by 2¾in). Turn under 1.5cm (½in) along one longer side; press. Then fold the material in half

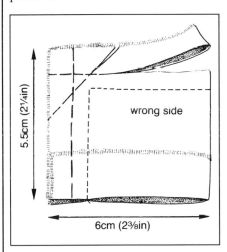

widthwise, right sides together and machine stitch along 2 sides, 1.5cm (½in) from the edge, leaving the edge with the turn-back open. Trim the seam to 8mm (¼in), and clip off the corner close to the stitching. Turn the binding right side out and slip it onto one end of the tie-back. Hand sew it firmly in place. Bind the other end in the same way.

9 Sew a ring to the back of the end of the tie-back just bound, so that it extends halfway past the edge. Bind the other end of the tie-back in the same way, and sew on another ring. Make the second tie-back in the same way.

Twisted tie-back

TWISTED TIE-BACKS
The twisted tie-back is very similar to a plaited tie-back, but only 2 tubes are used instead of 3. The twists are held together by being stitched to a stiff band. The twisted tie-back looks best when one of the tubes is in a contrasting colour.

The sample twisted tie-back
The tie-back used as the example in the following instructions has the same finished length as the sample plaited tie-back and is about 3cm (1¼in) wide when finished. The length of the strips for making the two tubes is determined in the same way as for the plaited tie-back (see page 112).

Materials for twisted tie-backs
The materials for the twisted tie-backs are the same as for the plaited tie-backs, with the addition of fusible buckram for the backing band. The buckram used is the same as the buckram used for hand-pleated headings.

Making twisted tie-backs
1 Follow steps 1–6 for making the plaited tie-backs (see instructions on page 116), but make only 2 tubes instead of 3.

2 Now make the buckram-interfaced backing for the tie-back. Cut a strip of buckram 60cm by 2.5cm (23½in by 1in). Cut a piece of material to match one of the tubes, measuring 63cm by 8cm (24½in by 3in). Machine stitch this strip and turn it right side out as for the other tubes. Slip the buckram into the tube, positioning the seam at the centre back. Fold the raw edges of the material to the inside at both ends and sew the ends together by hand.

3 Clamp the machine-stitched end of the tubes onto the edge of the table. Wrap the 2 tubes around each other and pin them together at the end. Now check that the tie-back is the desired length, measuring it 1.5cm (½in) from the raw edge at one end to 1.5cm (½in) from the raw edge at the other end (this allows for the turn-backs.) Unpin and trim one end if this is necessary. Then trim 2cm (¾in) off the end of the interlining inside each tube and machine stitch the ends together in the same way they were stitched together at the beginning of the twist (see step 6 on page 116).

4 Folding the seam to the wrong side (between the twists and the band) at each end, hand sew the twisted tie-back to the buckram-interfaced band.

5 Sew a ring to the back of each end of the tie-back so that they extend halfway past the edge. Make the second tie-back in exactly the same way as the first.

CATERPILLAR TIE-BACKS
Caterpillar, or 'ruched', tie-backs are gorgeous. They perfectly complement the ruched headings of curtains slotted onto poles (see page 62), as well as curtains or pelmets with a stand-up heading that has a ruched-band detail (see page 64).

Instructions are given for making three types of caterpillar tie-backs: simple caterpillar tie-backs, caterpillar tie-backs with 'ears' and caterpillar tie-backs with contrasting 'ears'. A caterpillar tie-back with 'ears' is a ruched tie-back which has a frill along both sides. All three types of caterpillar tie-back are very easy to make.

Caterpillar tie-back

The sample caterpillar tie-backs
The simple caterpillar tie-back used as the example in the instructions has a finished length of 60cm (23½in) and a finished circumference of 9cm (3¾in). Both of the sample caterpillar tie-backs with ears are the same length as the simple one, but they are about 6cm (2½in) wide when completed.

The length of the strip of material used to form the ruched tube depends on the type of material being used. When using chintz, I tend to cut the strips about 4 times the desired finished length. But silk requires about 6 times the final length of the tie-back to look sufficiently full.

The interlining is cut the same length as the finished tie-back and forms the core onto which the material is ruched.

If you want a thicker tie-back than the sample one, just make the tube wider. For a simple caterpillar tie-back, the interlining should always be cut nearly twice as wide as the tube material. For a caterpillar tie-back with ears, the interlining should be cut about 3½ times as wide as the finished width of the channel between the frills.

Materials for caterpillar tie-backs
The materials for the caterpillar tie-backs are the same as for the plaited tie-backs, with the addition of contrasting material if you are making contrasting frills.

Making simple caterpillar tie-backs
1 Cut a strip of material 12cm by 2.40m (4¾in by 7ft 10½in).

2 Make a single tube as described in steps 2 and 3 of the plaited tie-back.

3 Cut a strip of medium-weight interlining 17cm by 60cm (6¾in by 1ft 11½in).

4 Stuff the tube as in step 5 of the plaited tie-back (see page 116), but do not untie the string.

A thick plaited tie-back adds impact to this symmetrical French-pleated curtain design (left). The tie-back has been made with two contrasting colours to accentuate the plaits.

5 In order to ruche the material covering the interlining you must first secure the fabrics together at the opposite end from the string. Position the seam at the centre back, then machine stitch 1.5cm (½in) from the end of the tube through both tube and interlining.

6 Clamp the machine-stitched end onto the edge of the table. Holding the string firmly stretched out in one hand, ruche the tube onto the interlining (see diagram below) until it is pushed up just past the string knot. Undo the knot and slide the material back to line it up with the end of the interlining. Machine

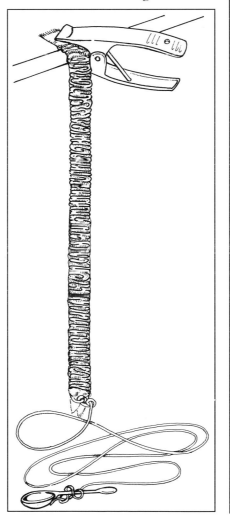

stitch across this end as for the first end of the tie-back. Even up the gathers along the interlining.

7 Now bind the ends of the tie-back. Cut a piece of material 7.5cm by 6cm (2⅞in by 2in). Placing right sides and raw edges together, machine stitch one of the wider sides of this rectangle to one end of the tie-back, centring it so that 1.5cm (½in) extends to either side and

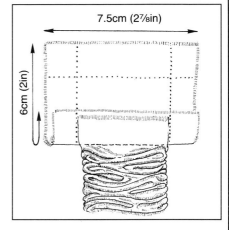

working the stitches 1.5cm (½in) from the raw edges (see below). Turn under 1.5cm (½in) on the remaining raw edges, and fold it in half over the end of the tie-back. Hand sew it in place. Bind the other end of the tie-back in exactly the same way as the first.

8 Sew on rings as for the twisted tie-back. Make the second tie-back in the same way.

Making tie-backs with ears
1 Cut a strip of material 16cm by 2.40m (6¼in by 7ft 10½in).

2 Make the single tube as for the tubes in steps 2 and 3 for the plaited tie-back.

3 Place the seam at the centre back, then press the tube. Using matching thread, topstitch 1.5cm (½in) from one edge along the length of the

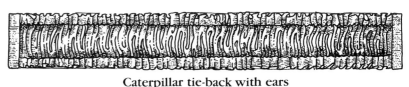

Caterpillar tie-back with ears

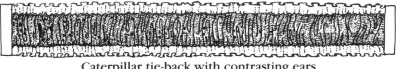

Caterpillar tie-back with contrasting ears

tube. Topstitch along the other side of the tube in the same way. This topstitching creates the stand-ups, or 'ears'.

4 Cut a strip of medium-weight interlining 12cm by 60cm (4¾in by 1ft 11½in).

5 Stuff the centre channel of the tube, as in step 5 of the plaited tie-back, but do not untie the string.

6 Follow steps 5–8 for the simple caterpillar tie-back to ruche the tube onto the interlining and bind the ends, but cut a rectangle 9.5cm by 6cm (3⅝in by 2in) for the binding.

Making contrasting ears
1 Caterpillar tie-backs with contrasting ears are made in much the same way as those with plain ears, but the tubes are made differently to incorporate the contrasting colour. Cut 2 strips of main material 7cm by 2.40m (2¾in by 7ft 10½in). Cut 2 strips of contrasting material 5cm (2in) wide and the same length as the other strips.

2 Placing right sides and raw edges together, machine stitch one contrasting strip to one main strip along their long edges, making a 1.5cm (½in) seam. Stitch the other contrasting strip to the other edge of the main strip. Join the remaining strip of main material to the free edges of the contrasting strips to form a tube. Stitch a temporary seam across one end. Trim the seams to 8mm (¼in).

3 Follow step 3 for the plaited tie-back.

4 Align the seams so that the main strips are superimposed on top of one another, then press the tie-back flat. Using a matching thread, topstitch along the seamlines just inside both contrasting strips. This

topstitching creates the contrasting stand-ups along the side edges.

5 Complete the tie-back as for the caterpillar with ears, steps 4–6, but cut a rectangle 10cm by 6cm (3¾in by 2in) for the binding.

BOW OR KNOT TIE-BACKS
The 'bow' or 'knot' tie-back has a heavenly, extremely soft appearance. The great secret in making this tie-back is to make 2 separate sashes to tie around each curtain. So instead of constantly tying and untying it, you simply release one ring at the

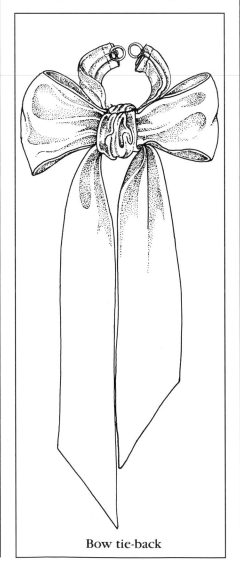

Bow tie-back

back. It is up to you how long to make the sashes. But my rule – LENGTH IS ELEGANCE – applies as always. The size of the sashes in the instructions are quite a good standard size.

All you need for this tie-back is a remnant of material. Interlining is not used, as it would hinder the crisp look of the finished bow and its knot.

Making the bow tie-back
1 Cut 2 strips of material 22cm by 1.10m (8½in by 3ft 7in).

2 Fold one strip in half lengthwise with right sides together. Beginning at the very end of the strip, machine stitch along the long side 1.5cm (½in) from the edge, ending 11cm (4¼in) from the other end; then turn the material 45 degrees and stitch diagonally to the fold, ending 1.5cm (½in) from the raw edge. Press to embed the stitches, trim the seam and turn the strip right side out. Turn in 1.5cm (½in) at the open end and hand sew the edges together. Press. Make the other sash in the same way.

3 At the straight end of one sash, make 3 or 4 pleats; machine stitch across them 1cm (¼in) from the end. Sew a ring to the pleated end

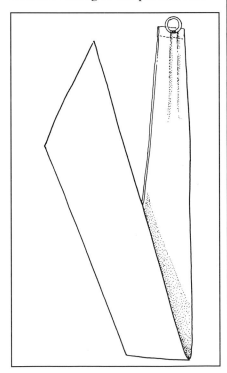

(see diagram on previous page). Finish the other sash in the same way. Then make two more sashes for the other tie-back.

4 Hook two sashes onto the tie-back hook at the side of the window, and bring them around the curtain. Tie the sashes together carefully. Do the same with the other tie-back.

ROSETTES, MALTESE CROSSES AND BOWS

Flower rosettes, choux rosettes, Maltese crosses and bows have been used in window treatments for over two hundred years. The earliest type of pelmet was merely festooned material above the window. Bows or Maltese crosses were stitched to the places where it was caught-up to form swags.

Where to use decorative details
It is important that you choose the right detail to complement exactly the inherent character of a window treatment. Rosettes, Maltese crosses and bows are most often used in the following situations, where they make a significant contribution to the overall design of the window treatment:

– At the top two corners of an Austrian blind
– On a caught-up pelmet
– At the centre top of a pair of ruched swags
– At the top centre of a pair of fixed-headed curtains
– On tie-backs

FLOWER ROSETTES

Flower rosettes have a lovely light and subtle quality. They are one of my favourite types of rosette. Made entirely by machine, they are particularly quick and easy both to make and to fix in place. They have the added advantage of a contrasting binding at both outer edge and centre. This is important if one is endeavouring to balance all the details of a particular window treatment which has a pelmet with a contrast-bound frill.

Size of finished flower rosettes
The flower rosette is made by gathering together a length of

contrast-bound set-on frill (see page 23). The flower rosette used as the example in the following instructions is made from a frill with a finished width of 8cm (3in) – this is about as large as this type of rosette should be. You can, if you wish, make flower rosettes smaller than this, using a narrower frill; but, if you do, you should use a slightly narrower binding.

Materials for a flower rosette
All you will need to make a flower rosette is a small amount of your curtain material, matching thread and a contrasting material for the binding.

Making a flower rosette
1 Cut a strip of main material 8 by 45cm (3 by 17¾in), using straight-edged scissors.

2 For the contrasting binding, cut 2 strips 4cm by 45cm (1½in by 17¾in), using pinking shears.

3 Place one contrasting strip on one edge of the main strip with right sides facing. Machine stitch them together 1cm (⅜in) from the long edge. Stitch the other contrasting strip to the other edge of the main strip. Press to embed the stitches.

4 Follow steps 4, 5 and 6 of the *Contrast-bound set-on frill* on page 24, but in step 6 do not fold under the beginning of the frill, and machine stitch just below the binding when gathering or pleating.

5 Placing right sides together, machine stitch the short ends of the

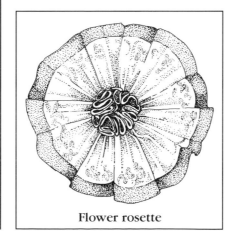

Flower rosette

frill together 1cm (⅜in) from the edge. Trim the seam, but do not press it open. Work a machine zigzag along the raw edge.

6 Thread a large needle with a strong double thread and knot the end. With your fingertips, bunch together the gathered or pleated side of the frill just under the binding. Holding the rosette pinched together like this, insert the

needle through the gathers just below the binding (see diagram above) and pull the thread through. Now wrap the thread 3 times around the rosette, again just below the binding. Fasten off.

7 The rosette is basically finished – the gathered edge forms the flower centre and the rest the 'petals'. But to form it into its correct shape you must now close it like a flower, pulling the frill up over the gathered centre and pinching it together so that it is wrong side out. Wrap a rubber band tightly around the new

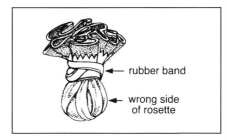

gathers just below the outer binding (see diagram above). Leave the rubber band in place for a day. When the rubber band is removed, the rosette will curve forwards forming a flower-like shape.

8 To fix the finished flower rosette to a caught-up pelmet, sew it in

place with a few hand stitches, or use a small tack which can be hammered into the pelmet board.

CHOUX ROSETTES

Choux rosettes have a particularly subtle and old-fashioned quality. Unlike flower rosettes, they are entirely hand sewn. The sample choux rosette in the following instructions is a good size for most requirements. It is 10cm (4in) in diameter. If you want to make a

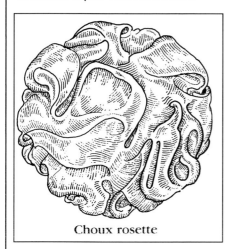

Choux rosette

smaller choux rosette, simply make its circular base smaller, and cut a square of material with each side measuring 3 times the diameter of the circle.

Materials for a choux rosette
To make a choux rosette you will need a small amount of each of the following:

– Curtain material (and matching thread)
– Fusible buckram
– Medium-weight interlining

Making a choux rosette
1 Cut a circle of fusible buckram 10cm (4in) in diameter. Cut 2 pieces of medium-weight interlining exactly the same size and shape. Place the buckram between the 2 pieces of interlining and press to fuse them together. Divide the circle into quarters on one side by

These bow tie-backs (left) are very soft and feminine; their look is totally un-contrived. The size of the tie-backs are just right for balancing the window treatment.

drawing 2 straight lines with a pencil through the centre (like dividing a pie). This will serve as a guide when gathering the material to the edge of the circle.

2 Cut a piece of material 30cm (12in) square.

3 You must now pleat the material onto the edge of the circular base, fitting one side of the material onto one quarter of the edge of the circle. Do not worry about making the pleats terribly regular. This does not matter at all, since they will not show when the choux is complete. (The choux will look much like a bathcap once the material is attached to the circle and before it is caught-down at random on the circle.) To begin, thread a needle with a matching thread and knot the end. You will also need a thimble. Fold 3 small pleats along one edge of the material (right side upwards), beginning 2cm (¾in) from one corner, working from left to right and about 1.5cm (½in) from the raw edge. Now with the 3 pleats in your right hand pick up the circle with your left hand so that the marked side of the circle is facing you. Fold

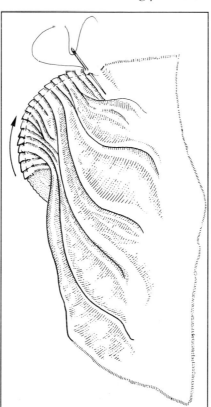

the pleats over the edge of the circle, placing them at the beginning of one of the 4 sections and folding 1.5cm (½in) of the material to the back of the circle. Holding the pleats pinched over the edge of the circle with your left hand, insert the needle from back to front through the first pleat, about 5mm (¼in) from the edge. Pull the needle through and reinsert it a little to the right and from back to front. Always working from left to right, work a few more stitches along the little pleats, making sure that the needle catches the circle with each stitch. Then with your right hand make a couple more pleats and fold them over the edge of the circle. Holding the pleats in place with your left hand, stitch them to the circle. Continue in this way, pleating the first side of the material onto the first quarter of the circle. Then pleat the next side of the square onto the next quarter of the circle, and so on. At the corners you will have to turn gradually onto the next side, starting about 2cm (¾in) from the corner. If, when pleating the fourth side, you have a little too much or too little material for the last quarter, this does not matter – just pleat it onto the circle as evenly as you can.

4 Once the material has been completely sewn to the edge of the circle, pull the material out over the edge all the way around. To pucker the material down onto the circular base (see below), use a matching thread and a thimble and catch it to

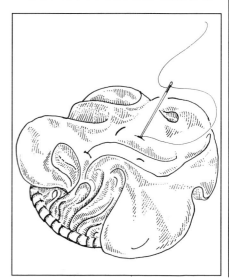

the circle with a few stab stitches. You can choose to make either a rather 'explosive' and uncontrolled choux rosette, which is caught down in very few places, or a tighter and more methodically arranged one, entailing more stitches.

5 To cover the back of the choux rosette cut a circle of material 13cm (5in) in diameter. Place it on the back of the circle, turn under the edges and pin. Slipstitch around the edge, then remove the pins.

6 Fix it in place just as for the flower rosette.

MALTESE CROSSES
The ultimate in elegance, the Maltese cross is highly suitable for reception rooms. It looks especially impressive on its own in the centre of the heading of a pair of fixed-head curtains.

The sample cross in the following instructions measures about 22cm (9¼in) across. Once you have learned the principle for making the

Very full choux rosettes like these (above) are made by using a larger piece of material than called for in the instructions on page 123.

Instead of buttons, little square patches of striped material have been placed at the centre of these Maltese crosses (facing page, top).

Well-formed Maltese crosses in a subtly contrasting colour add impact to these fixed-head curtains (facing page, bottom).

the other end in the same way. Press to embed the stitches, trim the seam and turn the sash right side out.

3 Turn in the open edges, and hand sew them together. Press.

To tie the bow
1 Hold the sash with one-third of it folded down as shown left.

2 Wrap the longer section from right to left (see arrow in step 1) around the front of the top of the sash above your left hand, ending as shown below.

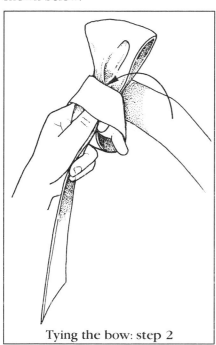

Tying the bow: step 2

3 To form the left hand loop of the bow, push the longer section through the 'knot' at the front as shown by the arrow in step 2.

4 Pull both loops of the bow from their back section to tighten the knot. If you pull from the front you will merely shorten the sash without tightening the knot. Arrange the ends of the sash so that both points fall on the inside (see finished bow on the facing page).

5 To attach the finished bow, either stitch it in place or staple the back section of each side of the bow to the pelmet board.

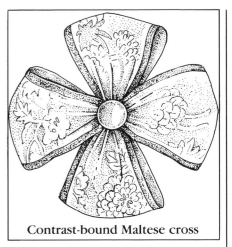

Contrast-bound Maltese cross

cross you can make a larger or smaller one as desired.

Materials for a Maltese cross
In order to keep the cross light and crisp, do not use interlining. For a simple Maltese cross all you will need is a remnant of your curtain material, matching thread and a 2.5cm (1in) button mould to make a covered button. For a cross with contrasting edges you will also need a piece of contrasting material.

Making a simple Maltese cross
1 Cut a strip of material 26cm by 47cm (10in by 18½in) – this is called strip A. Cut a second strip 26cm by 45cm (10in by 17¾in) – this is strip B.

2 Fold strip A in half lengthwise with right sides together. Machine stitch 1.5cm (½in) in from the long edges. Trim the seam, press to embed the stitches and turn the strip right side out. Move the seam to the centre of one side and press flat. With the seam on the outside, slip one short open end 1.5cm (½in) inside the other short end and machine zigzag over the raw edge. Make up strip B in the same way as strip A.

3 Take B and turn the ring of material inside out so that the seam joining the short ends is on the inside of the ring. Flatten the ring with the short seam at the centre of the back and pinch the centre together into pleats to form a bow shape. Using a matching thread, sew these pleats in place. (Do not worry

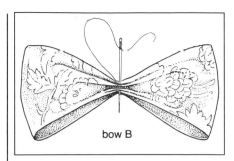

bow B

45cm (
contras

3 With
togethe
materia
side 1.
Then fo
remain
pieces
press to
the tub
seams :
is form
strip; p
ends to
facing,
in) from
in the s

about the zigzag seam at the back, as it will never show.)

4 Repeat step 4 using A, but instead of pleating both sides together, pleat each side separately as shown in the diagram below.

4 Comp
simple

When r
treatme
long st
form a
made u
parts w
The size
persona

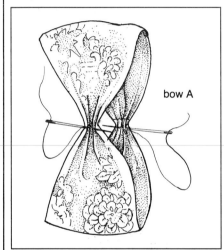

bow A

5 Slip bow B inside bow A, and sew them together at the centre.

6 Make a covered button and sew it to the centre of the cross.

7 Stitch the cross in place on your window treatment.

Making a contrast-bound cross
1 A contrast-bound Maltese cross is made in much the same way as the simple Maltese cross already explained, but the strips for the bows are made to incorporate the contrasting colour. Cut 2 strips for A – one measuring 13cm by 47cm (5in by 18½in) in the main material, and the other measuring 16cm by 47cm (6¼in by 18½in) in a contrasting material.

2 For B, cut 2 strips – one 13cm by 45cm (5in by 17¾in) in the main material, and the other 16cm by

Mak
1 Cut a
(6in by